Ho Chi Minh

a biographical introduction

Ho Chi Minh

a biographical introduction

Charles Fenn

Charles Scribner's Sons
New York

Contents

Acknowledgements

The author wishes to thank the following for permission to quote from their publications: Hoang Van Chi, *From Colonialism to Communism*, Pall Mall Press; Jean Lacouture, *Ho Chi Minh*, The Penguin Press and Editions du Seuil; *Cinq Hommes et La France*, Editions du Seuil; and Robert Shaplen, *The Lost Revolution*, Andre Deutsch.

Maps by Charles Fenn

1 Background

Faces all have an honest look in sleep.
Only when they wake does good or evil show in them.
Good and evil are not qualities born in man:
More often than not, they arise from our education.[1]

Until 1945 the country now called Vietnam existed only as part of the French Colony formerly known as Indo-China. This name of Indo-China, applied by the French to the total area they had subjugated, had a nebulous application. Except in regard to the Chams, a southern ethnic group whose culture reflects Hindu origins, Vietnam is neither ethnologically nor in any other respect associated with India. Ties with China there are, as we shall see: a long history of influence and domination. But this would no more justify the application of the word 'China' to the area than would, for example, the influence and domination of Russia *vis-à-vis* Finland justify applying to that country the word 'Russia'. Although the original Vietnamese may have come down from China, they have too long been a distinct people to warrant any Chinese label.

The French colony was formed out of five territories: Tonkin in the north, Annam on the coastal strip, Cochin China[2] in the south-east, Cambodia to the south-west and Laos in the far west. Of these five, only Cambodia and Laos may be said to have existed as separate communities: mountains, rivers and impenetrable jungles helped to keep them so. Tonkin, Annam and Cochin China, on the other hand, having easy communications both by land and sea, have tended to be homogeneous and unified. They were made effectively so when the Emperor Gia-long, at the end of the 18th century, brought them under his supreme rule and gave to the total area the name of Vietnam, an ancient appellation meaning roughly 'land of the far south': that is, south of China. When the French conquered this area during the 19th century they established a central government in Hanoi to administer the whole of Indo-China, thus lending the territory a further unity. This is important to remember when we later consider the artificial division into 'North' and 'South' Vietnam.

The French realized that, despite some ethnic and cultural differences, Vietnam, Laos and Cambodia formed a geographical strategic unit. The Annamese chain of mountains and the Mekong river extend through the whole peninsula from north to south and can be compared to the backbone and the main arteries of the human

---

[1] The poems at the head of each chapter are from Ho Chi Minh's *Prison Diary*. See page 71 and Appendix B.

[2] Here again the appellation 'China' is irrelevant. The name 'Cochin' was a corruption of a native term. As there was already a Cochin in India, the French added 'China' to distinguish.

body. United, the three countries become complementary to each
other....[3]

Having dropped the name of Vietnam (perhaps because it reminded
the inhabitants of their recent independence) the French marked on the
map the vague divisions of Tonkin, Annam and Cochin China, and
called all the inhabitants 'Annamese', although it would have been
equally sensible to call them 'Tonkinese' or 'Cochinese'.

The French colonial administration, while creating a union for the
sake of administrative and military convenience kept its five colonial
dependencies in Indo-China politically apart and fostered a feeling of
hatred between the Vietnamese, the Cambodians and the Laotians
and even between north and south Vietnam.[4]

The subjugation of Cambodia, Laos and the Cochin China area was
comparatively straightforward; but Annam and Tonkin presented
formidable resistance, not being finally conquered until 1885. To
counter the enormous French superiority in weapons and trained men,
these north Vietnamese utilized the guerrilla tactics for which they were
later to become famous. Thus, an historian of the period relates how

the occupation became a prolonged warfare, in which 25,000 French,
compelled to guard innumerable posts, had to oppose an intangible
enemy, appearing by night, vanishing by day, and practising
brigandage rather than war.[5]

Most of Vietnam lies within the tropics; the rains are heavy, the vegeta-
tion lush. In the valleys grow cotton, cocoa, coffee, tea, sugar-cane and
tobacco, as well as more exotic crops like sesame, indigo and cardamom.
But rice is incomparably the most important crop.
   The area is dominated by two rivers, both flowing down from the
Chinese plateau in the north. The lesser, called Red river, from the
earth that muddies its waters, alluviates the rice delta of North Vietnam.
In the south, the prodigious Mekong, third largest river in Asia,
alluviates a delta so large, in a soil so rich and a climate so humid, that
at least two rice crops can be grown within the year, and this area
formerly offered the largest export of rice in the world. It was thus vital
for North Vietnam's more urban and industrial population.
   The mountains are extensive, with ranges of Alpine grandeur. The
jungle is wild, lush and untameable. On the fringes, tigers, panthers and
leopards – all rapidly dwindling in a world no longer fit for wild
creatures – compete for deer and boar dwindling equally fast, or get
lesser meals from still-plentiful monkeys. The natives hunt for the
almost-extinct rhinoceros, whose horn, communism or no communism,

---

[3] Hoang Van Chi, *From Colonialism to Communism*, Pall Mall Press, 1964,
   p. 12.
[4] *Ibid.*, p. 13. Note, however, that this is a Vietnamese speaking; ethnic and
   cultural antagonism in Indo-China pre-dated the French.
[5] De Lanessan, *La Colonisation Française en Indo-Chine*, 1895.

in war or in peace, still makes the favourite love-potion from Peking to Singapore. Elephants have almost disappeared. But in the broad reaches of the Mekong you can still find crocodiles twenty feet long and giant fish weighing two hundred pounds. Except in a few urban centres, Vietnam does not yield easily to civilization's bulldozers.

On the other hand, under colonialism, rulers and ruled alike seem fated to get tarnished. The rulers become mercenary, arrogant, contemptuous, intolerant, and some become ruthless. The ruled become servile, indolent, crafty, treacherous; and some become rebellious. It is when the rulers become particularly ruthless that the ruled become particularly rebellious.

The art of ruling successfully seems to lie in the ability to exploit the subject nation without ruthlessness, and thus get the most out of it with the least disharmony. In Vietnam, certainly, the French were not able to meet this requirement. Unfortunately for them the Vietnamese were inherently resistant to being ruled, having already had a long and sometimes successful experience in keeping the Chinese at bay; and the country lends itself to that type of guerrilla warfare in which a poorly armed peasant population can deploy itself against overwhelming odds.

The more the natives resisted, the more the aggressor felt constrained to ruthlessness. In Vietnam – as in, for example, Ireland[6] – a paranoiac hatred built up – alongside a genuine admiration for the 'mother country'. The Vietnamese, of course, had less chance to discover the real France than the Irishman had to discover the real England. But some did go to France to study, while others met Frenchmen, even in the Colonial service, who were not corrupted. These Vietnamese thus became aware of French virtues as well as of French vices. The Mekong delta may give two rice crops a year, but in the art of living, said George Herbert, 'France is a meadow that cuts thrice a year'. There has always been something about the French way of life – divorced as it is from either Anglo-Saxon stiffness or Middle-eastern sensuality – that appeals strongly to the Asian.

Thus we find in Vietnam, and particularly in the northern part where Ho Chi Minh was born and brought up, a population potentially and even actively rebellious; disliking the French to a point of hatred while yet nurturing a genuine admiration and esteem for that France beyond the narrow world of colonialism. This curious ambivalence we need to keep in mind if we wish to understand the character and role of Vietnam's Lenin.

We also need to take into account the influence of China. According to tradition, this influence goes back at least three thousand years. It was about 1000 BC that the tribe of the Giao-chi, then inhabiting the provinces of Kwangsi and Kwangtung in southern China, made their way down along the coastal strip of what is now Vietnam; and having taken root, were slowly transmuted, by cross breeding with indigenous tribes and other competitive invaders as well as by the effects of climate and food, into the subsequent Vietnamese.

[6] See P. J. Honey, *Communism in North Vietnam*, M.I.T. Press, Boston, 1963, p. 88.

In the 3rd century BC the Chinese invaded the country in force; and having overwhelmed the comparatively sparse population, then maintained an intermittent supremacy for six or seven centuries. They called the country An Nam, meaning 'pacified south' (that is, south of China). This term survived as applied to the central coastal strip (Annam) although it had originally included Tonkin and parts of Kwangsi and Kwangtung.

A century later we find the first use of the name 'Vietnam' ('distant south'); but this name was not in general use until reintroduced by Gia-long two thousand years later.

The long Chinese domination resulted in a significant sinocization. The Buddhist religion prevailed over the former animistic cults, Confucian ethics replaced the primitive codes of a tribal society, and Chinese characters were adapted to the Vietnamese spoken language. This last development in particular gave China and Vietnam an indissoluble bond, since through the subsequent centuries every educated Vietnamese has necessarily understood written Chinese and thus been heir to the rich store of Chinese culture. Finally, and politically most significant, the Chinese system of officialdom, the so-called Mandarinate, was introduced, whereby competitive examinations of an academic and cultural nature produced the Mandarins who formed the civil service. This was of advantage in producing officials of scholarly distinction, free from economic and political pressure; but it also offered the disadvantage of establishing a hierarchy resolutely opposed to changing the *status quo*, since any change might threaten their own security of office. Such unyielding conservatism fails to meet the challenge of social, economic and political change. The country thus becomes vulnerable not only to internal dictatorship but also to foreign intervention.

With the collapse of the Chinese Tang Dynasty in the 9th century AD the Vietnamese at last ousted their Chinese overlords, only to find themselves torn apart from internecine strife. Amongst the contending groups were the aforementioned Chams, who were now driven into the wildernesses of the southern jungles.

During these struggles the Chinese found further opportunities for invasion. It was not until the 15th century that the warrior Le Loi effectively pushed them north again; and proclaiming himself emperor, established the Le Dynasty, which lasted uneasily for three centuries. The Chinese were dissuaded from further incursions by repeated tributary offerings; but internal dissension between rival groups of mandarins kept the country divided. These struggles finally merged into a dual contest between the house of Trinh in the north and the house of Nguyen in the south.

These latter, from their centre of operations in Hué (later to become a dynastic city), slowly expanded south and west into Cambodia, where the Mekong delta offered the rich rice lands. This expansion brought them into contact with those European nations – France, England, Portugal and Holland – already competing for economic privileges further west. The Nguyens concluded treaties, particularly with the French, permitting their privileges to be extended into Vietnam. In return the French gave vague promises of help in the Nguyen military adventures. Various factions of the Mandarinate opposed these French incursions. Periods of toleration alternated with periods of intense xenophobia. Frenchmen and all those natives flirting with either Christianity or Western commercial enterprises risked (and often suffered) execution. This led to French reprisals.

In the midst of this uneasy flux (towards the end of the 18th century) the Nguyens were overthrown by internal rebellion, the so-called Tay Son revolt, led by three brothers (also Nguyens!) who not only put the ruling Nguyens to flight but defeated the Trinhs in the north as well as a Chinese invading force. This brought a new unity to Vietnam. But the brothers' efforts having exhausted their resources they found themselves unable to oppose the energetic Nguyen prince who subsequently became the Emperor Gia-long. Singularly enough, he accomplished his victory with French help. A certain Pigneau de Behaine, Bishop of Adran, wanting to promote both his country and his religion, introduced a Trojan Horse into Gia-long's ultimately unfortunate domains. Unable to get official support, the Bishop had nevertheless persuaded part of the French garrison in Pondicherry (then a French post) to make the 3,000-mile voyage across the Indian Ocean and round the Malayan peninsula, in order to assist with the reorganization of Gia-long's forces. France and the Christian Church were rewarded with privileges that put them safely ahead of their European rivals – and effectively sealed the doom of Vietnam independence.

In the 1840s, one of Gia-long's successors, Tu Duc, becoming aware of this impending doom, took measures against the French, who then staged a naval invasion and later sent a task force to occupy the south. This was the beginning of steady encroachment. When, some thirty years later, the French got as far as Hanoi, Tu Duc, still struggling, appealed to the Chinese for help. But the Chinese troops who were sent to his rescue found they were no more a match for French barbarians in Haiphong than they had been for English foreign-devils in Canton. France consequently proclaimed a protectorate over the whole of Vietnam and the inhabitants were effectively muzzled for the next sixty years.

Those of us old enough to look back at the colonial era remember with a kind of bewildered unease that for the most part we accepted this muzzling of Vietnamese, Africans, Indians, Burmese, Indonesians and other subject races as part of the general pattern of organized society. If we happened to be Englishmen, Frenchmen, Germans, Dutch, Belgians or Italians, we took as much pride in boasting of our 'possessions' as we take today in boasting of our 'gross national product'. We were satisfied that Africans, for instance, were lower in the evolutionary scale; and that Asiatics, although entitled to be called *homo*, could scarcely be described as *sapiens*. One has only to remember the names applied to the rulers (baas, master, sahib) as against the single pejorative given to the ruled (native). Originally a useful term to describe an indigenous person, this finally classified its recipient with a status only one step up from a dog.

This is, of course, only one side of the coin. There were good things as well as bad. Many colonial servants strove genuinely for the welfare of the natives. Nor can it be forgotten that, even before the French came, Vietnam was anything but well-run. The standard of living was for the most part desperately low, taxes bore heavily on the peasant, the

Mandarinate generated and maintained an unapproachable élite, and
the emperor exercised despotic power. But people are more inclined to
accept such abuses from their own kind than from foreigners. In the
Far East this became particularly significant. If in Napoleon's army
every soldier carried a field-marshal's baton in his knapsack, so in China
and Vietnam every peasant carried an emperor's sceptre tucked inside
his carrying-pole. It is a curious fact that in these countries where
political democracy did not exist, social democracy (a concept that
'there but for the grace of God go I' – whether up or down the scale)
was more real than in western countries. Fate makes the emperor; fate
can also unmake him, and substitute the peasant. That was the belief,
however naïve in substance. Colonialism broke down such belief:
obviously when the 'emperor' became a ruling foreigner, no peasant
had a hope of taking his place. This is one reason why a despotic native
was resented less than a despotic foreigner.

The French, furthermore, broke down the whole tradition of Vietnamese social life, which was based, first on family authority, second
on the village community, third on Confucian principles, fourth on
Mandarin justice, and fifth on Imperial rule. All this was inherent,
traditional, understood, and for the most part accepted: at heart people
are all children and like best *to know where they stand*. The French
disputed family authority because it interfered with their own. In regard
to village life, urban-minded French officials misunderstood its importance and undermined its influence. Confucian principles were dis-
couraged in favour of a code to suit the French. The Buddhist religion
was made secondary to Christianity. The Mandarinate, left to handle
only minor affairs, nevertheless found themselves supervised by petty
French officials. Short of throwing up their job they had to conform;
all too often this meant corruption, indolence and indifference, plus the
added penalty of being classified in compatriots' eyes as French
collaborators. As for the emperor, he grew to be accepted as a tool of
French exploitation.

The pattern of this exploitation was much the same as elsewhere:
trade followed the flag in Saigon as in Singapore, Mombasa, Calcutta
and Hong Kong. But Indo-China did not offer the plums that had once
been so easily gathered. The slave trade was finished, there was almost
no ivory, no hoard of past treasures, no precious stones, sparse mining,
and a comparatively limited population among which to exploit cheap
labour. The consequent struggle for profits tended to make the French
more aggressive and potentially ruthless. This behaviour turned cheap
labour into rebellious labour.

Meanwhile the breakdown of the family, the village, the Mandarinate
and similar checks against social decline, turned some of the labour
source into mere vagrants, who invaded the growing urban centres in
pursuit of casual employment, charity or crime. To take up the slack,
as well as to ensure their own organizational control, the French insti-
tuted public works: roads, barracks, bridges, harbours, fortifications.
But a great deal of this was forced labour. The entrepreneurs meanwhile
built factories. Those natives who got jobs at first thought themselves
well paid as compared with their former earnings as peasants. But they
soon discovered the truth of the American quip that 'a dollar on the
farm is worth ten in the pay packet'. With urban growth and rural

decline, the cost of living always leaps ahead of pay packets. Nor were there yet any trade unions to remedy this.

The French, not a race to give up easily, struggled hard against these odds. By the turn of the century the economy had largely resolved itself into a *modus vivendi* whereby French private investors controlled all the manufacturing, mines, rubber plantations and general import-export, the Bank of Indo-China controlled the currency and finance, the Chinese community controlled rice exports (largely to China) plus the retail trade, and Vietnamese economic aspirations were limited to agriculture. With such small pickings for the Vietnamese hierarchy it was inevitable that they should exact high rents and even higher interest on loans to tenant farmers. Thus increasing numbers of peasants were driven off the land and into the towns.

There is one advantage that urban workers gain over their rural compatriots: whereas farming is usually an isolated occupation in which every man must fend for himself (whether against the elements or against human exploitation), town employment means mass employment. The urban worker soon finds a thousand others who share his grievances. At the turn of the century 'workers of the world unite' was a cry that had long shaken Europe, but was only now to impinge on Asia.

The French drove one more nail into their colonial coffin by introducing French education in place of the Chinese-orientated schooling. They thought this desirable not only for their own purposes but for the benefit of the deprived native, who would now, as far as possible, be taught the French language as well as his own. It was also decided that in written Vietnamese a romanized transcription in place of the Chinese characters then employed would make the language far easier to learn, thus encouraging literacy (see Appendix A.)

The result of French interference in Vietnamese education was that, not having enough teachers for any general instruction of the population, those peasants who had formerly received simple schooling now got none. When the French took over there were tens of thousands of village schools, albeit each with only a single teacher and conducted in a cowshed. These were substituted for some considerable period by French schools or French-orientated Vietnamese schools to be numbered in mere hundreds. From a Western point of view the quality of the teaching went up; but from any point of view the spread of learning undoubtedly went down. Moreover, the French overlooked the threat inherent in the end-product: the Vietnamese educated in French schools, inculcated with French thought, and wanting to occupy places inside the French hierarchy (whether socially, economically or politically), found themselves excluded from any chance of equality. They consequently became a resentful anti-French élite.

Meanwhile, their compatriots educated in the French-type Vietnamese schools were disgruntled for different reasons: having become acquainted with the roman alphabet they were able to learn and read French without much difficulty. This opened up to the more ambitious a whole new world in which they could discover, for instance, through French translations of Marx and Engels, not only that workers of the world *should* unite, but how this would enable them to get free from their masters. Unlike their French-schooled compatriots they did not aspire to be equal with the French, they aspired only to get rid of them.

When later on they read Lenin they learned that there were Westerners actually ready, not to say able, to support them in this aspiration. This call for international action gave the Vietnamese rebel a powerful boost. He felt his struggle was no longer isolated. He felt impelled to seek out these revolutionary sympathizers.

He also learned from Lenin that it was not enough to be a nationalist; it was not enough to protest; it was not even enough to revolt. First you had to organize, to form *cadres*, to enlist recruits, to spread propaganda, to infiltrate the Establishment, the Press, the trade unions (where existing) and the army. Above all you had to ally yourselves with the workers and the peasants.

Such was the Vietnam Ho Chi Minh was born and brought up in. No doubt he, like most great leaders, was born out of the social, economic and political pressures of that time and of that place; thus being not only the product of his parents' genes but of the environment and broader circumstances that conditioned his childhood. Let us examine those parents and that childhood and endeavour to assess their relative influence on the product.

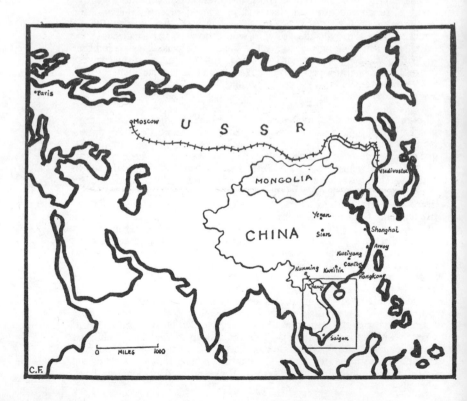

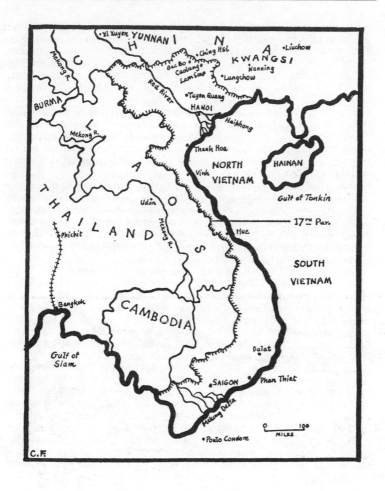

2 Child

Wearily to the wood the birds fly seeking rest.
Across the empty sky a lonely cloud is drifting.
In a village in the mountains, a young girl grinds out maize.
When the maize is all ground, the fire burns red in the oven.

The name of Ho Chi Minh is one of many pseudonyms. He was born
Nguyen Sinh Cung and his father's name was Nguyen Sinh Sac. In
terms of numbers, the Nguyens are the Smiths of Vietnam. But unlike
our own Smiths, the Nguyens have been aristocrats almost as generally
as commoners. Ho's own Nguyen antecedents were for the most part
in the middle ranges; there were, indeed, several members of the family
who graduated as mandarins. But Ho's father, Sinh Sac, having been
the son of a concubine rather than of a first wife, found himself lower
in the social scale than his elder half-brothers.

Nevertheless Sinh Sac did manage to attend the village school. In the
hamlet of Sen where he was born (in Nghe An province near Vinh in
northern Annam), such school consisted of one-shack, one-teacher. At
some point early in Sinh Sac's tuition, his teacher decided to go back to
his native place, the nearby hamlet of Kim Lien, where he had inherited
a small farm. Needing a boy to look after the buffaloes he took Sinh
Sac along with him. In between his farm chores, the boy continued to
pick up a smattering of education and proved not only a proficient
pupil, but sufficiently well liked by the teacher and his family to win the
eldest daughter in marriage. Considering that Sinh Sac was, in effect,
no better than a paid hand, this was a useful step up. With the boss's
daughter went a ricefield and a bamboo mat-shed: a pleasing dowry.
'A woman under a roof' is the Chinese character for 'good': and a ricefield forms part of the character for 'happiness'.[1]

In this mat-shed in Kim Lien (now reconstructed to form a shrine for
the faithful) the young couple eked out a living and procreated three
children: a son, Khiem, a daughter, Thanh, and finally on 19 May 1890[2]
the third son then called Cung (in full, Nguyen Sinh Cung) destined to
be first President of his country.

Even into adult years and parentage, father Nguyen kept at his
studies and in 1894 passed the competitive examination that was the
first step to a mandarin's degree. For further study and examinations it
was then necessary for him to go to Hué, the royal city 250 miles south.
When father Nguyen at last managed to organize this formidable
journey with his wife and three children, Cung was seven or eight years
old. At that time there was no railway between Vinh and Hué.

Along the three-hundred-kilometres road through five provinces,
now going through crowded streets and villages, now climbing up

[1] See Appendix A.
[2] The date now given in official records.

high mountains, the youth's eyes and mind were much widened. Cung began his studies, but the greater part of them did not come from books. Together with his elder brother and some friends Cung used to go on excursions. A friend of his, whose father was a mandarin, had a baby pony and they liked to ride it. During a flood they made a raft with banana-trunks and went on pleasure trips. Usually they wandered from one longane-tree to another. Hué had so many things never seen in Chua and Sen villages. There were high fortresses, big houses and French soldiers who seemed to be always drunk. There was also a bridge spanning the Perfume river.[3]

A year or two later, in connection with certain examinations, father Nguyen was sent to Thanh Hoa, some 350 miles north. While he was gone his wife died in childbirth. Cung, having been the youngest child, was particularly attached to his mother. To lose her when he was only ten years old and his father was so far away must have presented a challenge that matured him beyond his years. Such deprivation may also have given him a special awareness of suffering, soon to become evident in his concern about the misfortunes of his compatriots.

Father Nguyen hurried back to rescue his three offspring; and having transferred them to their grandparents in the maternal village, went on to Hué to sit for the royal examination. Despite the recent stresses he gained a doctorate of the second degree. It was about this time that, following the general practice, he gave Cung a new name: Nguyen Tat Thanh.[4] Since his sister's name was also Thanh and this might cause confusion I shall continue to call him Cung.

In 1901 father Nguyen was due to take up his official mandarin post in Hué as secretary to the Ministry of Rites. But the new doctor had already found this prospect distasteful. He had discovered that the Mandarinate had become only a tool for French ambitions; and that worse than being a slave was to be a pander. Nguyen was not so much a rebel as a dissenter. In today's society he would probably veer towards the militant bloc of the National Union of Teachers. As things were, he registered his political protest by staying out of Hué and finding a convenient local school where he could impart to his pupils a certain amount of unorthodox teaching. But French officialdom at last forced him to take up his designated position. After a few years he was classified as something of a trouble-maker although not considered dangerous enough to be put behind bars. He was finally shunted off to a post as local magistrate in an isolated district 300 miles south. But it wasn't long before the French official supervising the area discovered the new magistrate's deplorable leniency towards culprits breaking laws of French origin. Nguyen was either dismissed from the service or given the chance to resign.

For some reason or other he decided not to return north or even at this period to re-establish contacts with his children. We find him

[3] *Days with Ho Chi Minh*, Foreign Language Publishing House, Hanoi, 1965, p. 22. Any biographer of Ho finds himself largely dependent on this source for Ho's early life. I have endeavoured to restrict my quotations to useful and non-controversial material.
[4] Cung means 'Respectful'. Tat Thanh means 'Who will Inevitably Succeed'.

wandering over much of South Vietnam and – perhaps from scholarly interest – getting as far as Angkor Wat. In Saigon he appears to have picked up a living prescribing medicines as well as from itinerant teaching: an example of a man who, having launched his family, chose to opt out of a society he found fraudulent. Thus, for at least his last twenty years, he was able to seek the kind of life he preferred.[5]

Before returning to young Cung, we may briefly consider the other two Nguyen offspring. They seem to have taken a more militant stand than their father in helping insurgent causes. The girl, Thanh, for instance, while billeting Vietnamese troops attached to the French garrison, succeeded in purloining their weapons for the use of the rebel nationalists. Another time, on the pretext of conducting family affairs, she smuggled weapons out of Hué for similar use. For this offence and others she was intermittently gaoled. After the declaration of Vietnamese independence in August 1945, recognizing with astonishment her younger brother's picture in the newspaper, she went to greet him in Hanoi, taking a gift of 'two ducks and twenty eggs'. Then she returned to her village and lived there until her death nine years later.[6]

Brother Khiem walked even more boldly along the rebel path. Starting out modestly by writing to the French Governor-General, Albert Sarraut, complaining of abuses, he then went so far as to resist a French official who kicked him, by pulling his aggressor to the ground. Although we have no record of the punishment meted out to him for this, it probably resulted in the first of his many periods in gaol. Most of his later offences were connected with more subversive activities.

The Vietnamese writer, Hoang Van Chi, gives a slightly different account of the family: according to him, sister Thanh was engaged to a young man who was sent to the prison-island of Poulo Condore, where he died. It was because of grief that she never married anyone else. As for brother Khiem, Chi calls him 'a mediocre student who failed in all his examinations'. This writer also has him going off in 1945 to meet his brother after thirty years separation. 'Ho was still anxious to keep his identity and background a secret. So instead of receiving his brother in the Presidential palace he sent him to a relative in the suburbs, where they later had an hour's talk, parted and never met again.'[7]

Whether or not this meeting ever took place, we have other evidence that Ho did not keep close ties with his brother. When Khiem died in 1950, Ho sent the following telegram to the village community:

> I am very sad at the news of my eldest brother's death. Very busy with state affairs and because of the long distance I could not attend to my brother when he was ill and now that he is dead I cannot see to his burial. Alas! I am guilty of lack of devotion to my brother's soul and beg my relatives and friends to forgive a man who has sacrificed his family feelings for state affairs.[8]

[5] *Days with Ho Chi Minh*, pp. 17/18.   [6] *Ibid.*, p. 19.
[7] *From Colonialism to Communism*, p. 37.
[8] *Days with Ho Chi Minh*, p. 40. In cutting himself off from his family, Ho has offered ammunition to his critics. His admirers on the other hand might say that the great Eastern teachers (including Jesus) advocate such severance by example if not also by precept.

No doubt because Nguyen *père* had become disillusioned with the Mandarinate he did not thrust any systematic education on his children. This particularly applied to Cung, the youngest, who seems to have used his ability to read not so much as a means of learning Confucian texts as an excuse to explore any book he could lay his hands on. It was thus very early in his life that he began to acquire the wide sweep of interests which would later put him at ease in no matter what part of the world or in what spheres of interest.[9]

In between periods of study, Cung was fond of playing the local variety of chess, or more energetically climbing mountains, which were formidable enough in these parts.

As he was growing up there were other things besides studying and playing. In the five-room hut built by the villagers, the two brothers occupied the fifth room next to the kitchen. In this room there was a wooden bed by the window. On hot days a hammock was hung in the room. From the window one could see the far-away Chung. Quite near, on the left, was Dien's forge which resounded with hammering all day long. On the right was the Coc well. In the old days the insurgents of Chung village threw their broad-bladed swords in this well when the enemy arrived, and fished them out after his departure. Nearer, right in the garden, were a few tombs among the lemon and shaddock trees.

The writer then develops this agreeable theme with darker overtones:

What occupied his mind then was the *corvée* forced upon the people by the French to build the Cua Rao highway which was intended for the 'pacification' of the country and Laos and the exploitation of our natural resources. The pain that grieved him this time was more serious than that from his mother's death. From the sad plight of *corvée* he deduced other miseries that daily took place around him. Taxes were increasing and the people lived in utter poverty. . . . His mind went back to the pompous life at Hué, the spring trips in great state by the King, and the elaborate ceremonies. Something had certainly got to be done to lead his relatives and villagers out of this hellish existence.[10]

Since Cung was still only ten years old it seems unlikely that his mind was actually occupied by these adult problems; especially since, his father being a mandarin, his own family was exempt from *corvée*. Ten-

[9] In this respect Ho outclassed other top political leaders, for he not only read about other countries and visited them, he made a point of learning their languages. He spoke Vietnamese, French, English, Russian, Siamese and at least three Chinese dialects, in addition to having a working knowledge of several other languages. I once heard him go first from French to English to help with a technical point, then explain the matter to his companion in Vietnamese and finally address our Chinese radio operator in fluent Cantonese, almost as it were, in one breath.

[10] *Ibid.*, pp. 25–8.

year-olds, whatever their subsequent genius, are unlikely to preoccupy themselves more with the misery of others than with the anguish of a mother's death. Nevertheless, we may be sure that in such an environment

> Shades of the prison house begin to close
> Upon the growing boy. . . .

It was not only the forced labour on projects destined to be used against the natives' own interests; there were rack rents, rural indebtedness, crippling interest rates, high taxation, government monopolies and the overall decline in human dignity that always comes with foreign suppression. To this picture a French writer adds further grim details:

> . . . the massive conscription of northern coolies, to provide labour for the plantations and estates of Cochin China; the spread of the sale of alcohol; the readiness to turn a blind eye to the taking of opium; the efforts to raise troops for service in Metropolitan France; the marked tendency to 'take advantage' of the young ladies of Hué or Cantho. And Poulo Condore, that small penal settlement in the Indian Ocean where a living death was meted out. . . .[11]

Nor was it likely that Cung, even as a child, would fail to be aware of the protests and organized uprisings of his adult compatriots and of the consequent French reprisals. A great deal of this revolutionary clamour reverberated in the immediate area of his birthplace, the province of Nghe An, which might well also be called the birthplace of nationalism, so repeatedly had it procreated revolutionists. At the very outset of French suzerainty, the mandarin Phan Dinh Phung staged his famous 'Scholars' revolt'. This was followed by a succession of uprisings, all put down with reprisals that the French called salutary and the natives called savage. In 1901 (Cung being then eleven), another mandarin, Phan Boi Chau, who had graduated as First Laureate in the recent royal examination and was a celebrated poet, organized a coup to seize control of all the local towns. He staged this uprising for Bastille Day, when the French military were likely to be occupied more with celebrations than with guard duty. Nevertheless the French got wind of it, took instant counter measures and made wholesale arrests. But they failed to capture Phan Boi Chau, whose destiny it now was to bring Cung himself into the revolutionary movement.

After his failure with the Bastille Day coup, Phan Boi Chau set up a new revolutionary society called the Hoi Duy Tan (the Modernist Movement), in which an hereditary prince named Cuong De, who had already taken an anti-French stand, was nominated president. In his attempt to undermine the French, Cuong De proposed enlisting the support of all the foreign interests to which he had access. As things turned out, only the Japanese proved both willing and able to translate verbal sympathy into useful action. Their support was not due to altruistic motives, but in order to assist their evolving policy to extend Japanese influence amongst all Asiatic peoples, as a balance against the

[11] Jean Lacouture, *Ho Chi Minh*, Allen Lane The Penguin Press, 1968, p. 6.

encroaching Western powers. In other words Cuong De, instead of using the Japanese, was to be used by them.

In 1906 Phan Boi Chau went to Japan and returned full of enthusiasm for what they had to offer. Under the auspices of the Modernist Movement he began recruiting young enthusiasts for study in Japan; and Cung, then about fifteen, was one of those selected. This invitation must have exerted an enormous appeal to a boy looking outwards from his own provincial world and anxious to become associated with an important revolutionary movement. Furthermore, Phan Boi Chau seems to have had a magnetic personality that usually won people over. Why, then, did young Cung decline the honour thus done to him? According to one of his early friends, Thanh Tinh, it was because 'He felt, though not very clearly, something wrong with Mr Phan's policy of reliance on powerful mandarins to kindle the fires of the royalist movement, of advancing a prince as the standard bearer of the uprising and chiefly of reliance on Japanese aid.'[12]

One suspects, however, that this rejection of Phan's offer contains a more significant clue to the youth's character. Thanh Tinh reveals that the invitation had been prompted by Nguyen *père*, who was a friend of Phan's.[13] Cung would be consciously or unconsciously rebellious to his father's lead. As the younger of two sons (both with positive personalities) he would, according to our present psychologic concepts, be inclined to dispute authority, opt out of the family and particularly resist a father who had (in the eyes of a boy of ten) gone away and let his mother die. The fact that his father had later on left his offspring to shift for themselves is also suggestive of a break in relationship.[14]

It was soon after this episode with Phan Boi Chau that Cung showed his mettle in a more positive way and as a consequence had his first recorded brush with authority. The French provincial governor, in an attempt to break up Phan's subversive activities, summoned all the local mandarins and scholars with a view to grilling them. Cung's father being then off in Hué, the governor ordered the mayor of Cung's village to present himself as a surety. Cung promptly delivered himself up in the mayor's place. Either the governor lost face at this action of a mere boy or he decided that such an action deserved a generous

---

[12] *Days with Ho Chi Minh*, p. 30. Whether or not Cung was really so prescient, his subsequent history certainly confirms this mistrust of Japan. When the Japanese took over Indo-China in 1941 Ho was as much against them as he had been against the French. Indeed, although he often proved willing to co-operate with Frenchmen against the Japanese intruder, there is no evidence of his ever co-operating with the Japs against the French.

[13] But Lacouture implies that Cung's father advised against going to Japan. *Op. cit.*, p. 10.

[14] Here is a typically restive, almost refractory youth, quite in line with today's much-abused teenagers who break away from home, refuse to settle at any one thing, appear aimless, are against authority whether in the family or society, long to travel, and are willing to put up with any amount of dirt and discomfort in the process. So Cung continued until he was at least 25. Then it was almost as if, like Joan of Arc, he heard voices, which told him that he, and he alone, was destined to be the saviour of his country: he suddenly stops his wanderings, becoming totally dedicated.

response. Cung was not only allowed to depart but the mayor was left in peace.

Soon after this episode, Cung went off to study in the secondary school in Hué. The curriculum was essentially French-orientated, and the teaching staff either French or pro-French Vietnamese. The head-master, a certain Logiou, had actually served in the French Foreign Legion. This in itself made a Spartan régime inevitable. But it happened that M. Logiou had further qualifications as a despot: having on one occasion been a prisoner of certain nationalists who treated him with something less than tenderness he now found splendid opportunities to get his own back. Cung was thus subjected during his four years at the school to a very special sort of conditioning. This encouraged him to enter more and more actively into revolutionary affairs, and particularly in the widely extended revolts of 1908, in which many top Vietnamese patriots were either imprisoned or executed.

In 1909, when Nguyen *père* was sent off from Hué to the far south, Cung seems to have felt he could now escape from his disagreeable life at school: giving up further studies he went off to a teaching job – also far south, even further than the area his father had gone to, the fishing port of Phan Thiet, 100 miles due east of Saigon. One might guess that Cung was glad to put himself within easy reach of an international port from which shipping went regularly to every part of the world. There was even the advantage of a railway which traversed the hundred miles of jungle between Phan Thiet and Saigon in a few hours. A more imme-diate reason for choosing Phan Thiet, however, was that Phan Boi Chau got him a job there as teacher in the Duc Thanh school.

> On the southern bank of the Phan Thiet river, some kilometres from the sea, there were then a few little houses with wooden bars as walls and where it was cold when the wind blew from the sea. Duc Thanh school was one of those. The school belonged to the Lien Thanh Company, which produced fish sauce and sold groceries. The fish sauce factory and the grocery shop were situated on the river bank some distance from the school which was subsidized by profits from the business. The school and the company had both been set up during the Modernization Movement in previous years. In the then situation these were patriotic deeds aimed at opening the people's minds and encouraging practical trades. . . . Teacher Cung taught French and Vietnamese in the second and third forms.[15]

Then a curious thing happened. Although it may be supposed that Cung now found himself in a sympathetic environment (and many of his pupils later confirmed this fact), he suddenly, after only eight months in the school, disappeared without warning. No one seems to know why. Did he come under pressure from the French, did he anticipate the forced closing of the school (which happened not long afterwards) or did he simply feel some imperative need to take a new step? The Dr Chi already quoted gives the date of his leaving as 'one Monday morning in October 1911' and suggests that the Chinese nationalist revolution of that time may have had something to do with it.

[15] Dr Nguyen Kinh Chi, reported in *Days with Ho Chi Minh*, p. 36.

This particular revolution, which overthrew the imperial dynasty and established an enduring republic for the first time in Chinese history, has traditionally been considered to have started with the mutiny of troops in Wuchang on 10 October 1911 (the cabalistic tenth day of the tenth month, usually celebrated in China by both Left and Right). It is possible that this news coming via telegraph to Saigon would have reached Phan Thiet in a matter of days and thus prompted Cung to leave the same month. Certainly such news, which must have been anticipated and discussed for weeks, was not only the biggest event in Asia since the Manchu invasion but for nationalists of the period would have had the same electrifying stimulus that the Russian revolution was later to have on Western socialists.

Certainly for Cung, now twenty-one years old and matured beyond his years both by study and experience, this event had special significance. Able to read Chinese from an early age, he was almost as well acquainted with Chinese history as with that palimpsest of Vietnamese history on which China had for thirty centuries printed an indelible record. And he would hope to find in Saigon a vast pool of overseas Chinese ready to support his own nationalist ambitions.

There is, however, no evidence that he did contact these Chinese nationalists. This move to Saigon, like the move to Phan Thiet, may have resulted more from chance than from fixed purpose. Certainly, Cung's conduct at this time seems erratic. Having arrived in Saigon he went back to studying. This time, however, he chose a technical school: one set up by the French to train skilled workers in various branches of commerce and industry. Since this training was essential to the growing French economy, promising students were awarded scholarships. There is evidence that (with no political pressures or police interference) the general atmosphere was tolerant. The period of tuition was three years but Cung stayed only three months. Perhaps by now he was determined to get out of this stifling environment where 'natives' were inevitably subservient. In Saigon he would have learned from those who had travelled abroad how easy it was to sign on articles that would get him to France in a mere six weeks. This may have been why he turned his back on the technical school.

Having changed his name to Ba (presumably because the police already had him listed under his own name) he signed on as assistant cook in the *Amiral Latouche Tréville* of the *Compagnie des Chargeurs Réunis*. This job would not have called for any qualifications: the designation 'assistant cook' covers all those unskilled workers who peel potatoes, scrub out the galley and run and fetch between the storeroom and the pantry. The *Compagnie des Chargeurs Réunis* plied between Indo-China and the home port of Marseilles, with innumerable calls *en route* according to cargo requirements. The term '*Chargeurs*' suggests that the ships were essentially freighters, although there would also have been passengers, 1st, 2nd, 3rd, and even 4th class, crowding every inch of space. Conditions of work would have been grim. When the ship was on the high seas and the captain became king, the crew, mostly natives, would be little better than slaves. 'To the discerning man, education is a bagful of gold. But hardship is a sackful of diamonds.'[16]

[16] Seneca.

It was about Christmas, 1911, when the *Amiral Latouche Tréville* steamed down the Saigon river and out into the South China Sea. Cung, alias Ba, would have looked back towards his native shores less with regret at leaving them than with excitement at the adventures lying ahead. He could hardly have expected that he wouldn't see those shores again for thirty years.

3 Novice

Only when out on the road can we take stock of our dangers.
After we climb one mountain, another looms into view:
But, once we have struggled up to the top of the mountain range,
More than ten thousand li can be surveyed at a glance.

There is no major political figure of the 20th century about whose early
life we know so little as we do about Ho's. Whole years present us with
an almost total blank. Although he wrote continually, the output was
either journalism or polemics; there are no diaries,[1] and almost no
surviving letters. Thus, the record of his years at sea is limited almost
to the bald statement that 'he went to France, then round Africa, to
England and America, visiting many countries in Europe'.[2] The one
person to explain why, having arrived in France (which was presumably
his original goal) he then went off to sea again, is Hoang Van Chi who
explains[3] that Cung had first gone to Saigon to see his father and get
advice as to the best means of helping his countrymen throw off their
yoke. Nguyen *père* had consulted with his revolutionary friends and it
was decided that Cung should be sent to Paris to make contact with
insurrectionists there and more especially with a certain Phan Chu
Trinh with whom Nguyen *père* had been incarcerated on Poulo
Condore.[4] Phan himself had recently gone to Paris under the wing of
a rebel group called The League for Human Rights, who would also
offer Cung help. According to Hoang Van Chi, Cung did make contact
with Phan in Paris but 'found him too ready to co-operate with the
French'. It was because of this disillusionment that Cung left Paris and
went back to sea, sailing extensively to European, African and American
ports, and at least on one occasion re-visiting Saigon.[5] Hoang Van Chi
further states that on this occasion Cung went to see his father to tell
him what had happened in Paris. The old man, having already been
notified by Phan of the boy's perfunctory behaviour, went for his
ungrateful son with a stick. Cung at once rejoined his ship, and father
and son never met again.[6] This information is important only as a clue
to Cung's staying at sea for two whole years. On the other hand, what
young man, of an imaginative and curious bent, does not yearn to see
as much of the world as he can?

During Cung's voyages to America he sailed into New York, and the
writer can here offer a personal comment. Some thirty years later he

[1] Other than *Prison Diary*, which consists of poems expressing emotions
rather than facts. See p. 71 and Appendix B.
[2] *Days with Ho Chi Minh*, p. 38.
[3] *From Colonialism to Communism*, p. 36f.
[4] A detail not mentioned elsewhere.
[5] *Ibid.*, p. 37.
[6] Hoang Van Chi, a former associate of Ho's, but later a confirmed opponent,
relates these details as if from hearsay and gives no source.

mentioned to me that the American War of Independence (called in
America The Revolutionary War) had inspired his early thinking. Sailing into New York harbour, he had looked at the Statue of Liberty
with mixed feelings, the French having made a considerable *réclame* by
presenting it to the American people under the pompous title of *Liberty
Enlightening the World*. But New York City in general, with its sky-
scrapers, bridges and subways[7] impressed him as the prototype of
Western progress. Ho told me how he and a shipmate made a long and
to them adventurous journey from the dock in Hoboken to Manhattan
via ferry and then in an electric street car towards Chinatown, where
they had talked in Cantonese to migrants who still spoke hardly a word
of English. What had stood out in his mind was that all these Chinese
living in the heart of a Western capital and surrounded by millions of
Westerners nevertheless had equal rights and privileges in law if not
always in fact.

Towards the end of 1913, after roughly two years seafaring, Cung
went ashore at Le Havre for good and thus ended his career as a
seaman. In the neighbouring watering-place of Sainte-Adresse, he got
a job as gardener, perhaps to get some funds in hand. Shortly, we find
him crossing the Channel and arriving in London, where he gets work
as kitchen hand in the old Carlton Hotel. Nobody knows why he went
to London rather than to Paris. Perhaps his shipmates had told him
that what was then the world's largest capital offered splendid opportunities for meeting everyone connected with political intrigue. This
seems to be confirmed by the fact (according to Hoang Van Chi) that
he soon made contact with the Overseas Workers Union, recently
established by Chinese and Indian workers. We do not know whether
he contacted any British left-wing groups, or whether he was yet
sufficiently acquainted with Marxism to visit Marx's grave in Highgate.
But at one point we hear of his visiting Liverpool, where he was in
touch with Irish nationalists, shortly to stage the Easter Rising (1916).
Returning to London, he apparently found the Carlton Hotel glad to
have him back: it seems that Escoffier, then Chef, had been impressed
by this boy who spoke good French and was also deft with his hands.
Cung was thus promoted to the pastrycook's larder.[8]

These were the years of World War I: horribly grim years in London,
with severe shortages of food, severe bombing by Zeppelins, and all
services strictly curtailed by pressures of war. But perhaps Cung also
found them exciting years. There was a spirit of cameraderie, nowhere
more evident than in London, thanks largely to that Cockney cheerful-
ness which seems to bloom in adversity. Especially for leftists were

[7] The Metropolitan Life Insurance Building, just completed, was then the
eighth wonder of the world; already three of the East River's spectacular
bridges had been built, including the largest, the Manhattan; the subway
system included tunnels beneath mile-wide rivers; while the palatial Grand
Central and Pennsylvania railroad stations were revolutionary both in
concept and function.

[8] Bernard Fall, *Le Viet Minh*, Librarie Armand Colin, Paris, 1960, p. 24. The
author adds that Ho enjoyed this work and was always a gourmet at
heart. This seems doubtful. Ho enjoyed good food in company but at heart
he was essentially an ascetic.

there new stirrings of militancy because vastly increased employment in factories meant a consequent expansion of the trade union movement.

But there came a time when Cung, having learned the English language and something about left-wing politics, felt he should move on to an area more directly concerned with Vietnamese problems. The war had gone into its third tragic year and France, bleeding and desperate, had imported tens of thousands of Vietnamese to serve not only in the army but in every form of civilian capacity. Cung would thus have access to a body of compatriots who would not only be working together in groups (and therefore thinking and operating collectively) but would also have a chance to discover what Cung himself had discovered on board the *Amiral Latouche Tréville*; namely, that French 'superiority' is confined only to a section of the French population. In Vietnam (as in every other colony) the policy of the French hierarchy had been to convince the native of his inferiority *vis-à-vis* the civilizing master-race. But now these Vietnamese troops were fighting in the trenches alongside the French, with nothing to be thought of except kill or be killed. One soldier was equal to any other soldier; and corpses went into the same mass grave. When a regiment of French troops mutinied there were even Vietnamese amongst the military police ordered to fire on them. Natives shooting at their omnipotent masters made nonsense of French superiority. Meanwhile, the Vietnamese working in the factories found themselves alongside Frenchmen getting much the same pay for the same hours; and what was even more astonishing, being treated, if not quite as equals, at least as human beings.[9]

When Cung got to Paris and installed himself in shabby lodgings in the Rue Marcadet and then at 6 rue des Gobelins[10] he took a new name. Readopting his patronymic of Nguyen he added Ai Quoc, meaning 'love one's country'; in other words, Nguyen the Patriot. This was to be a name that for fifteen years filled an ever-expanding file in the French *Sûretè* (police security). Through his contacts with other Vietnamese patriots he soon got to know several important French left-wing intellectuals who not only treated him as an equal but even made much of him. The reason for this was not only that this poetical-looking Asiatic won their minds and hearts but that during the war 'Overseas France' had taken on a new significance: it having become essential to secure the co-operation of the colonies, all political groups tended to woo them. The Socialists were thus encouraged to favour all their Asiatic comrades.

In Cung's case he found himself drawn into a politico-intellectual society that was both a challenge and an inspiration. His outlook, his concepts, his grasp – all these broadened enormously. He began to understand, to appreciate and even to admire this France in which he was not only admitted into contemporary left-wing circles, but admired in turn. He thus escaped being prejudiced against Frenchmen as a race. He perceived that injustice was not merely between French master and native slave, but between the 'haves' and the 'have-nots' on an

9 See, for example, Bernard Fall, *The Two Vietnams*, Frederick A. Praeger, 1964, pp. 88/90.
10 Lacouture, *op. cit.*, p. 14.

international scale. He began to study Marxism and to learn that there was more in common between the French worker and the Vietnamese worker than there was between the French worker and the French capitalist. While he was learning these things from his new French friends, he found himself accepted as something of an expert on matters concerned with the Far East. He was thus in some respects deferred to by men at the top: Paul Vaillant-Couturier, editor of *l'Humanité*, the most famous of the communist newspapers: socialist Léon Blum, twenty years later to be Premier of France; Charles Longuet, nephew of Karl Marx, editor of the influential socialist newspaper, *Le Populaire*; socialist Marcel Cachin, leader of the extreme left that would soon become the French Communist Party: an extraordinary transition from the kitchens of the Carlton to these intellectual peaks.

As for Paris itself, Nguyen Ai Quoc (who will have so many more aliases that we had better now refer to him as Ho) was delighted with it, even though the conditions of his life there were something short of romantic. According to one report,[11] Ho had gone to France initially 'to interpret for [Vietnamese] coolie labour hired to dig trenches and latrines' but he was soon making a scratch-living retouching photographs. Lacouture quotes a classified advertisement from a leftist newspaper Ho was subsequently to work for, *La Vie Ouvrière* (Working class Life): 'If you would like a lifelong memento of your family, have your photos retouched at Nguyen Ai Quoc's. A lovely portrait in a lovely frame for 45 francs.'[12]

Ho himself says, 'I made my living in Paris, now as a retoucher at a photographer's, now as a painter of "Chinese antiquites" (made in France!)'.[13] The art of retouching photographs (mostly negatives), so essential to the beautified portrait human vanity requires, calls for skilful fingers: Ho's long experience in the kind of brushwork necessary for writing Chinese characters was no doubt particularly good training for this kind of work. But he was also to go into something more appropriate for a man who was to become a top political figure of his age. One of his compatriots, Nguyen The Truyen, invited Ho to join him in publishing the revolutionary *Le Paria*, organ of the Intercolonial Union, and afterwards to achieve a certain fame in the annals of left-wing propaganda sheets. They shortly started another publication called *Viet Nam Hon* (the Soul of Vietnam) which was aimed at sympathizers outside of France: copies were smuggled to the homeland with the help of Vietnamese sailors.

Thus launched into professional journalism, Ho now wrote his first major contribution to revolutionary literature: *Le Procès de la Colonisation Française*, a treatise of some 30,000 words. Whatever help Ho had with this essay the French text is of admirable clarity even though the material is not always concise. Ho begins with an examination of French overseas recruitment for the war which had then (1917) reached such a peak of unavailing slaughter that France was on the brink of

[11] Harold Isaacs, *New Cycle in Asia*, American Institute for Pacific Affairs, 1947, p. 169.
[12] *Ho Chi Minh*, p. 14.
[13] *The Path to Leninism*, in *Collected Works*, or in *Vietnam, History, Documents, and Opinions*, Penguin 1966, p. 37.

exhaustion. Desperate to widen her conscription net, she had reached out into her colonies. The recruitment of the natives had been called 'voluntary'; but Ho is at pains to show us that this word when applied to subject peoples had an elastic interpretation. Each French district commissioner directed the mandarins of his area to round up so many 'recruits' within a certain time by whatever methods he deemed necessary. Only those Vietnamese able to pay adequate ransom could escape what was in effect conscription. Relatives of conscripts who happened *dulce et decorum* to give their lives for the motherland were rewarded with licences to sell opium.

Thus the colonial government committed two crimes against humanity. Not satisfied to promote the vice of opium, they tied it to the victims of fratricidal butchery and rated life so cheaply that they thought this putrid recompense quite sufficient for the death of a loved one.[14]

He also cites, with savage irony, the occasion of a commission 'charged to organize a fête to collect funds towards a "Monument to Dead Annamites"'. There was to be a fair, a country dance and a garden-party. The attractions were to be numerous and variegated and would include the attendance 'not only of aviators but all the élite for miles around.' A buffet of magnificent splendour would offer satisfaction to the most exacting gourmet. 'We shall certainly show the dead Annamites,' concludes the brochure, 'that we know how to appreciate their sacrifice.'

Chapter Two deals with the monopoly-sale of alcohol, the pernicious effects of which were almost worse than opium, since the extent of indulgence was considerably wider. The usual drink of the natives had been rice wine; but even when they drank distilled spirit it had been from tiny cups poured from small stone bottles. By overt example and inferred precept the French themselves encouraged copious drinks from large and well-promoted 'commercial' bottles; and thus set a pattern amongst the French-orientated natives which then spread to the natives generally. Alongside this went the monopolistic manufacture of rice-alcohol given by the colonial government to a French company set up for that purpose (*Société des Distilleries de L'Indochine*),

whose products were so bad that the Vietnamese preferred to drink their own distilled alcoholic concoctions. To safeguard the French firm's interests, the government made frequent raids on Vietnamese property, imposing heavy fines and imprisonment. Despite these stringent measures, the private production of alcohol persisted. In the end, the government adopted the policy of distributing a fixed quantity of 'official alcohol' to every village, obliging the inhabitants to pay for it.[15]

Furthermore, this alcohol was always put into large-sized bottles to ensure a maximum invitation to excessive consumption.

[14] The quotations from *Le Procés de la Colonisation Française* are the author's translations from *Œuvres Choisies*, Hanoi, 1960, vol. I, pp. 195f.

[15] Hoang Van Chi, *op. cit.*, p. 39.

Ho's next chapter fulminates against French administrators in colonies as far apart as Dahomey and Cochin China. He builds up an overwhelming (and no doubt biased) case against 'these leeches who drain the colonies' blood, not only for the benefit of the mother-country but to grow fat themselves'.

Whether soup salesmen or school caretakers, once they get out to the colonies our civilizers live like princes. Each administrator uses five or six militiamen to look after his goats. Others utilize the militia to carve ornamental buddhas or elegant chests out of camphor wood. We find one official (entitled to a single militiaman) who employs
   1 commissariat chief, 1 *maître d'hôtel*, 3 waiters, 2 cooks, 3 gardeners, 1 valet, 1 coachman, 1 groom.
And madame enjoys: 1 dressmaker, 2 washerwomen, 1 seamstress, 1 basket-maker. The child has a special attendant who never leaves him. At meals every guest would have behind him a militiaman to attend to him personally, and the team would be controlled by a sergeant.

Chapter Four deals grimly with the particular method whereby the blood is drained from the native body-politic. It ends, however, on a cheerful note: the aspiring native is told how he can apply to become a French citizen, thus not only avoiding further drainage of his own blood but himself getting into the leech club. The choice of qualifications is set out clearly in the law of 25 March 1915:

1. To have obtained the Legion of Honour or a University or similar diploma.
2. To have given important services to colonisation or other French interests.
3. To have served in the French army and acquired the rank of officer or petty officer or have earned the Military Medal.
4. To have married a French woman and have acquired a dwelling place.
5. To have resided for at least ten years in the said country and to know sufficient French.

The following questions have also to be answered satisfactorily:
1. Do your wife and children speak French?
2. Do they dress in European style clothes?
3. Has your house got furniture?
4. And chairs?
5. Do you eat at table or on a floor-mat?
6. What do you eat?
7. Do you eat rice or bread?
8. Do you own any property?
9. And your wife?
10. What do you earn from your work?
11. Your religion?
12. What organizations do you belong to?
13. What is your role in these organisations?
14. Considering that the laws for natives are so favourable, why do want to be naturalized? Is it to get an official post? To enhance your position? Or to prospect in gold or precious stones?
15. Who are your most intimate friends?

A little bit more, adds Ho, and these gentlemen would want to know if our wife wipes our b . . . .

In another chapter Ho shows what native populations can expect from 'a Madame Justice who has had such a rough passage on her voyage to Indo-China that she's lost everything except her sword'. Further chapters deal with the stifling of the native Press, the suppressive role of the Church, and the particular crimes committed against the native women.

All of Ho's attack is delivered as if by an armchair anarchist. In denouncing the iniquities he is fairly wise if not always wisely fair. He endeavours to prove his accusations with facts. He knows something about history, about economics, about the political structure of the world, about human nature; and he knows that if you wish to sound reveille you most blow your bugle shrilly. But there is nothing in all this to indicate that the bugle call is from any political group. Neither Marx's nor Lenin's name appears in the whole 100 pages. Ho states the iniquities of colonial exploitation without relating them to the iniquities of capitalism; and communism is never once mentioned.

Meanwhile he continued to write both for *Le Paria* and for *Viet Nam Hon*. It is in this second publication that he finally (under the name of Nguyen Ai Quoc) published the Eight-Point Programme that he and Nguyen The Truyen had hoped to submit to President Wilson at the Versailles Peace Conference (1919). The Vietnamese demands were fully in line with Wilson's own Fourteen Points, and included: 'The right of self-determination; constitutional government; democratic freedom; equality of the law for Vietnamese and French; amnesty for political prisoners; freedom of the Press; freedom to organize and assemble; abolition of forced labour, the salt tax and forced consumption of alcohol.' How respectable, how modest, how entirely reasonable, such demands sound today! Yet at the time they were laughed away as preposterous by everyone in France except the Socialists, then a minority group. Ho never got nearer Wilson than the outer door. But the mere fact of any Vietnamese even *trying* to see Wilson, receiving support from French intellectuals, and airing his views to foreign delegates was enough to cause a stir. A fellow-nationalist, who knew Ho at the time, puts it this way:

The imperialists held the Versailles Conference to redivide the colonial market amongst themselves. Suddenly they were faced with the claims for self-determination for Vietnam made by Nguyen Ai Quoc. The French called it a bomb. We called it a thunderbolt. We were over-joyed. How could any of us refrain from admiring the man who stood up so courageously to make claims on our behalf? The name of Nguyen Ai Quoc thus had extraordinary attraction.[16]

This writer, like Ho, was a seaman on one of the ships of *Chargeurs Réunis*. In June 1919 when he arrived at Marseilles he heard not only about his countryman's astonishing *démarche* but also that 'in Russia there was a socialist revolution, Lenin and proletarian power. Who

[16] Bui Lam in *Days with Ho Chi Minh*, p. 46.

were the proletarians? But I myself was one! And I felt at once tied to
the Soviet Union and grew bolder.' This sounds naïve, mere leftist
dogma; but we should try to understand it if only to understand Ho.
We need to imagine ourselves into the circumstances. At this point in
history, the whole of East Asia except Japan was in bond to the
Western powers. India (with Pakistan), Burma, Malaya, Indo-China
and Indonesia were fully subjugated. China and Thailand were in semi-
colonial strait-jackets. Every Asian (except the Japanese) was thus born
into a world that sooner or later presented him with the *fait accompli* of
Western domination. As with the dark-skinned races, he would sooner
or later find himself face to face with a 'white' human being who not
only intended to put him in his place but was able to call forth all the
necessary power to enforce such arrogance.

The Asians met this challenge in a variety of ways: the Indians, for
instance, with the shield of religious fanaticism; the Burmese with the
gentleness of Buddhism; the Chinese with the dignity of Confucian
ethics. In Vietnam the population reflected a mixture of all these
elements and added something of its own: an inherent resistance to any
kind of foreign domination. The Vietnamese, ostensibly gentle and non-
aggressive, physically slight, almost delicate, philosophically inclined
towards Confucianism, religiously inclined towards Buddhism, and for
the most part totally ignorant of Western concepts, found themselves
unable to understand either how or why a mere hundred thousand
Frenchmen had been able to rob ten million Vietnamese of their freedom; how or why some of their own countrymen had leagued themselves with the subjugators; and how and why their continuing efforts
to shake off the yoke achieved nothing but harsher repression. This was
how they saw things, regardless of French intentions, which were
sometimes good as well as bad. Then came the Russian revolution; and
Lenin not only identified his objectives with downtrodden people
everywhere, he offered active help. This was why Bui Lam 'felt tied to
the Soviet Union and grew bolder'. Soon he was reading *Le Paria*, where
articles signed Nguyen Ai Quoc

> roused me as if a fire were burning in my head. I dashed out to find
> some of my fellow countrymen and we read to each other. Tears
> came to our eyes. How could the short and concise articles so much
> rouse up the heart and soul of those who had lost their country, of
> the oppressed and exploited toilers? They urged us to action! But we
> were at a loss as to what was to be done. It came to our minds that
> we had to see Nguyen Ai Quoc.[17]

Bui Lam is elected by his shipmates to be an emissary. He sets off from
Marseilles and arrives in Paris armed with a copy of *Le Paria*, which he
thinks every Vietnamese will recognize.

> After leaving the railway station, whenever I met a yellow-skinned
> man I held out *Le Paria* and asked the way. I thought that any such
> men were sure to be colonial people and must know *Le Paria*. I
> succeeded in making my way to Marché des Patriarches Street in the

[17] *Ibid.*, p. 48.

6th district. The office of *Le Paria* was in front of a small market, and comprised two small rooms. Some North Africans were busily working, opening envelopes and writing.

But since on that particular day Nguyen Ai Quoc was not at the office Bui Lam pursued the trail to his home:

I arrived at Gobelins Street, looked for number six and went to the first floor. My heart beat quickly. I knocked at the door. Footfall, and the door opened. A man about thirty, tall, thin and pale, stood smiling before me. I remember his remarkable big and bright eyes. I followed him inside and at once felt at home. It was a single room with very simple furniture. A table stood in a corner, plenty of newspapers, magazines and books. Nearby were an iron bed and a small wardrobe.

On the next meeting (a Sunday) Ho took him along to an art exhibition:

Truly I was then very young and did not enjoy the visit. But it was a pleasure to be with him. There were hundreds of pictures and a very big crowd at the exhibition. Nguyen was well-known there. Many people came to shake hands with him or nodded greetings. He looked at the pictures very carefully, exchanging comments with his French friends. His comments showed that he had a good knowledge of art and French culture. [After a simple meal in a Chinese restaurant they go back to Ho's room.] Nguyen unrolled his mat on the floor, put two piles of books as pillows, then we both lay down to have a rest. He told me about his living. In the morning he made portraits for a shop on piece-work and earned just enough to live from hand to mouth. His life was even harder than ours who were paid a monthly wage. Yet he managed to save a part of his earnings for the printing of books and *Le Paria*. In the afternoon he worked at *Le Paria* office, writing and correcting articles. He also wrote for other newspapers and magazines such as *l'Humanité* and *Vie Ouvrière*. In the evening he went to clubs to take part in debates on philosophical, economic, political, social and cultural matters, or to the National Library. Besides this, he attended meetings of the street cell of the French Communist Party. Though very busy he always went out for a walk or visited exhibitions on Sundays. On my next journey to Paris he again took me to an art exhibition and to the Louvre Museum.[18]

Bui Lam also tells us how Albert Sarraut, the former Governor-General of Indo-China and then the Colonial Minister, on one occasion summoned Ho to his office. 'Clenching his teeth, the minister thrust out his hand, closed it and made a twist meaning that he wanted to smash his opponent, saying: "France has enough power to punish her adversaries." '[19] Yet it would appear that Sarraut took the opportunity to get a police-file photograph of this opponent he wanted to smash. 'It shows him with a small hat perched on top of his head, looking delicate and

[18] *Ibid.*, pp. 49–53.
[19] *Ibid.*, p. 56.

unsure of himself, a bit lost, a bit battered, like Chaplin at his most
affecting.'[20] Louis Arnoux, chief of the Indo-Chinese secret police, adds
that Ho was a 'slight young man with an enormous forehead, who
moved with a certain jerkiness as he handed out leaflets denouncing
colonialism in the most violent terms'. Nevertheless he appears to have
rather liked this fire-eater 'who spoke so poignantly of his village, his
family, his country, and of the injustice that had been meted out to his
father'.[21]

In 1920 Ho made a significant step forward when he took part in the
Socialist Congress at Tours. The big issue at this particular gathering
was in regard to the acceptance of the 'Third International' recently
promulgated by Lenin. As this complexity of 'Internationals' comes up
in various connections we need to know the background: the First
Communist International, inspired by the Communist Manifesto of
1848, was founded in London in 1864. But the failure of the Paris
Commune of 1871 showed that it was no good having a spontaneous
uprising without prior organization and ultimate central control. In
1889, therefore, a Second International endeavoured to remedy this,
with representation in all Socialist and Labour movements such as trade
unions, cooperatives, political parties and educational bodies. But as
time passed this body devoted more and more of its time and energy to
prevention of the war that was building up amongst the European
powers – a war that would bring only suffering and slaughter to the
working classes. When in 1914 the war broke out despite their frenzied
opposition the Socialists were thrown into confusion as to what path
to follow. Those who felt they should patriotically follow their country
into war were wildly denounced by other Socialists as traitors to the
working class. Meanwhile Lenin (then in Switzerland) had been advocat-
ing a new and more militant approach towards achieving the Socialist
revolution foreseen by Marx, and upon the outbreak of the war he
exhorted Socialists not only to come out against the war but to *utilize it*
as a way to achieve civil, i.e. class, war. In 1917 the Germans, seeing
in this an opportunity to sabotage the Russian military machine,
smuggled him back to Russia. The revolution having begun, the Third
International was founded soon afterwards.

The Communist International is the organization of the Communist
Parties of each nation; it is therefore revolutionary. Its chief purpose
is to accelerate the development of events towards world revolution.
It rejects any compromise or co-operation with bourgeois parties.
Similarly it rejects parliamentarianism as a normal method of political
development. In certain circumstances it advocates a unity of front
with Socialist parties, including the Second International.[22]

[20] Lacouture, *Ho Chi Minh*, p. 16.
[21] *Op. cit.*, p. 16. This mention of some special injustice to Ho's father would
appear to confirm the story by Hoang Van Chi that the old man had been
imprisoned on the island of Poulo Condore. See p. 25.
[22] And also with the '2½' International, a somewhat pejorative term for certain
breakaway socialist parties such as the Independent Labour Party in
England. The quotation is from the article on the Third International in the
Encyclopedia Britannica, 13th edition, 1926.

In the report of the proceedings at the Tours Congress, as published in *l'Humanité*, Ho is designated as Nguyen Ai Quoc, although in the official transcript he is merely 'The Delegate from Indochina'. There is a splendid photograph of the young Ho (which was published in *l'Humanité*) showing a gentle young Asiatic looking almost pathetic in comparison with beefy French delegates. In the photograph Ho is clearly speaking without a script, which suggests that he made the following speech impromptu, testimony to his already lucid French:

Ho: Comrades, I would have preferred to come here today to work with you towards the task of world revolution, but it's with the utmost sadness that I come, as a socialist, to protest against the abominable crimes committed against my native country.

As you know, French capitalism came to Indo-China half a century ago; and in the name of capitalism it subdued us with bayonets. Since then, not only have we been shamefully oppressed and exploited but even more hideously martyred and poisoned. I underline this word poisoned, by opium, alcohol, etc. It's impossible for me in a few minutes to describe all the atrocities committed in Indochina by these capitalist bandits. The prisons, always more numerous than schools, are horribly overcrowded. Every native considered to hold socialist ideas is imprisoned and sometimes executed out of hand. That is so-called Indo-China justice. For out there we find two scales for measuring justice: the Annamites don't get the same treatment as the Europeans and the Europeanized.

For us, liberty of the Press or of speech don't exist. Neither are we allowed to form unions or associations. We have no right to travel or to emigrate. We live in darkest ignorance, for we haven't even freedom of education. In Indo-China everything possible is done to drug us with opium and brutify us with alcohol. [In the war] Thousands of Annamites have been killed, slaughtered wholesale in fact, in defence of interests which are not their own.

And that, comrades, is how more than twenty million Annamites are under French 'protection'. The Socialist Party must certainly take action on behalf of my oppressed compatriots.

Longuet: I have already intervened on behalf of the natives.

Ho: At the beginning, I asked for silence! (laughter) The Party should promote Socialist propaganda in all the colonies. Joining the Third International is a clear promise of the Socialist Party to give the colonial question the importance it deserves. We were happy to learn of the creation of a permanent delegation for North Africa and we should be happy if the Party sent a specialist to Indo-China to study problems on the spot and decide what should be done.

A delegate: Like Comrade Enver Pasha?

Ho: Silence, members of the Party!

The President: And silence everybody else!

Ho: In the name of all mankind, in the name of all socialists, right wing or left wing, we appeal to you, comrades: save us! (applause)

The President: The representative of Indo-China can see from the applause that the Socialist Party is entirely with him in protesting against the crimes of the capitalists.

As the stage directions for this small drama are missing, the scene needs to be imagined: this young Asian, only three years in France, and still green in politics, addresses what might justifiably be called Europe's left-wing élite. It appears that he starts out by asking them for silence. This so intrigues these hardcore soapbox debaters that when he later gives them a reproof they can't but laugh at his cool self-possession.

The only reference Ho makes to Marxism or communism is in reference to the Third International; but it is a key reference. As already explained, it was at this Third International that Lenin expounded communism as a world revolutionary movement. We shall see later how Ho himself explains the special significance this had for colonial dissidents. He has now thrown in his lot with this Third International and wants to make that clear. But we see that Longuet, representing the right wing of the Party, and supporting the Second International (if only because he does not go along with Lenin) gets up to make a protest that his group already has the natives' interests at heart. Ho answers with what seems to be a sharp rebuke.

The final reference to Enver Pasha also has some significance. Enver, leader of a Turkish insurrection group *circa* 1900, went through some remarkable adventures before finally leading the Turks against the Russians in World War I. His campaign was a fiasco. Nevertheless, he subsequently busied himself with further exploits including a spell of *helping* Deniken against the Russian communists. He then *returns* to the Left as director of the Asiatic Department in the Soviet government and is sent to the Baku 'Congress of Oriental Peoples' as Chief Socialist Adviser. Hence someone's jeer when Ho suggests sending a socialist comrade to Indo-China. Not to be put off with irrelevancies, Ho again calls for silence.

One final aspect of Ho's years in Paris needs to be considered: his contributions to *Le Paria, Viet Nam Hon, Vie Ouvrière* and *l'Humanité*. He had been given space in this last publication by the editor, Paul Vaillant-Couturier, then and for years afterwards one of his most loyal supporters. As an example of Ho's contributions to this leading communist journal we may examine his *Reflections on the Colonial Question* (25 May 1922), in which he analyses the extent of the French colonies, and reveals the general ignorance of the French people concerning their vast populations and the prevailing indifference of the French government as to their welfare, an indifference that is broken only by periods of ferocious reprisals when the slaves make protests. 'The Gandhis and the de Valeras would have long since gone to heaven if they had been born in one of the French colonies' concludes the writer with the bitter sarcasm that characterized many of his utterances at this period.

In *La Vie Ouvrière* Ho wrote many articles that attack the iniquities of colonialism beyond the confines of the French Empire. This awareness of the conflict on an international scale reflects his gradual absorption of Leninism. The articles in *Le Paria* range widely, but a good proportion are scarifying indictments of French colonial exploitation and brutality or bitterly ironic 'open' letters to key colonial figures or the hierarchic fringe. When, for example, the Emperor of Annam, Khai Dinh, visited France in 1922 and was made a great fuss of, Ho's open letter ridiculed this hypocrisy: 'Apart from the racehorses at Longchamps and the pretty Frenchwomen at the Opera, what else has Your Majesty deigned to see in the course of Your instructive visit to the poetical land of France?' (Thereby nicely anticipating the behaviour of the subsequent Annamese Emperor, the better-known Bao Dai.) It was also with a view to satirizing this 'imperial dynasty' that Ho wrote a playlet entitled *The Bamboo Dragon*, apparently his one and only venture in this field. Vaillant-Couturier helped stage the piece, which had a modest *succès d'estime*.

As a final example of Ho's almost savage bitterness at this time (a bitterness that he largely eradicated in later years), we may take the following from *Le Paria*:

> When the soldiers arrived all the population fled except two old men and two women: a young unmarried woman and a woman nursing her newborn baby and holding by the hand a girl of eight. The soldiers first demanded money, brandy, opium. Becoming furious because nobody understood them, they then beat one of the old men to death with their rifle butts. After this, over a period of hours, two of them, already drunk when they arrived, amused themselves by roasting the other old man over a fire of twigs. Meanwhile, the rest of the group, having raped the two women, followed suit with the little girl; then, getting bored, murdered her. The mother having managed to escape with her baby into the underbrush, dared not move for fear of being discovered, and had to watch while the other woman was tortured to death; why, she didn't know; but the soldiers had pinioned her on her back, gagged her and then bayoneted her over and over again, the blade carving up her stomach with leisurely thoroughness until she was effectively dead. After which, they cut off her finger to retrieve a ring and her head to acquire a necklace. On the open stretch of salt-marsh the three bodies were left: the naked corpse of the little girl, the young woman disembowelled and with her right stiffened forearm clenched up into heaven, and the body of the old man: this one particularly horrible, naked like the others, distorted by the roasting, glistening with melted fat that had run out and congealed on the stomach, now scorched and gilded like the skin of a roast pig.[23]

This sort of atrocity story defies comment. True or false, such tales are the current coin of war propaganda. Ho probably judged his audience correctly. 'What men wish to believe, that they believe most readily.'

A French reply to such propaganda is given by one of Ho's opponents at the time, Governor Pasquier:

> 'I address myself to you, people of Vietnam, to your passive, credulous and tormented soul. Since there are those who, for anarchic and sacrilegious ends against your social and moral ideals, wish to nourish you with hate, utopias and lies, I in turn now address myself to you, peasant, worker, public servant, soldier, guardian of our hearths and homes, to give you a steady assurance that under the protection of France – powerful but benevolent – you may pursue in

[23] *Annamite Women under French rule, Le Paria*, 1 August 1922.

peace your progress towards a fruitful tomorrow. France will be generous towards you. But, for your safety, she will remain merciless to those anarchists who are enemies of her sovereignty.[24]

As against this, Ho's invective seems almost acceptable.

[24] Quoted by Henri Azeau, *Ho Chi Minh, Dernière Chance*, Flammarion, Paris, 1950.

4 Marxist-Leninist

The cocks crow once, the night is not yet over.
Slowly the moon climbs up the autumn hills
In company with the stars, but now the traveller
Who journeys far is already out on the road;
His face is beaten with icy gusts of wind.

Throughout Ho's career the question has been repeatedly asked: was he a nationalist or essentially a communist? Broadly speaking, we may say that liberals and leftists (excluding communists) prefer to think of him as a nationalist devoted to gaining his country's independence; whereas centrists and rightists consider him to be a communist.

But both amongst Left and Right, individual opinions often change. This is reflected, for instance, in a comment by an American writer, Herman Kahn. Postulating that the U.S. policy regarding Vietnam had been based upon the containment of communism, Kahn adds:

At the time President Kennedy made his particular commitment to South Vietnam it was reasonable for him to think of Ho Chi Minh as more of a communist than a nationalist, though today it is widely conceded that it may have been more relevant to view him as more of a nationalist than a communist.[1]

Ho himself says, 'I am a professional revolutionary. I am always on strict orders, my itinerary is always carefully prescribed; and you can't deviate *en route*, can you?' This is quoted by Robert Shaplen who adds: 'He surely meant it. But there remained the dynamic dream that has always been the passion of his life: a free Vietnam.'[2] We note, also, that Ho calls himself here a 'revolutionary', which could mean a nationalist. It seems a pity that Shaplen didn't ask *whose* 'strict orders'. At this period (1966) Ho could scarcely have been on strict orders from anybody, and he had no 'itinerary' except within his own country. The remark would, however, have applied well enough to his behaviour between 1925 and 1945.

The French scholar, Paul Mus, quotes Ho to show a different slant: 'When I was young I studied Buddhism, Confucianism, Christianity as well as Marxism. There is something good in each doctrine.'[3]

---

[1] *Can We Win in Vietnam?* (various contributors), Pall Mall Press 1968, p. 26. This opinion is confirmed by Charles B. McLane in *Soviet Strategies in Southeast Asia*, Princeton University Press, Princeton, N.J., 1966, pp. 214f. McLane adds that Ho never reconciled international communism with love for his own country.

[2] *The Lost Revolution*, Andre Deutsch, 1966, p. 40.

[3] *Vietnam, Sociologie d'une Guerre*, Editions du Seuil, Paris, 1952. Ho also gave Mus his description of American policy: 'Marshallization of the world'.

Expanding this particular comment Shaplen quotes another of Ho's statements: 'Everyone has the right to his own doctrine. I studied and chose Marx. Jesus said 2000 years ago that one should love one's enemies. The dogma has not been realized. When will Marxism be realized? I cannot answer. . . .'[4]

And Mus tells us that Ho cited the four virtues he considered as pre-eminent to be: *Diligence, frugality, justice and integrity*.[5] These particular virtues would come more within the concepts of stoicism; they might even be part of Confucianism, Buddhism or Christianity; they could never be accepted as of real significance in Marxism, which would probably put in first place *orthodoxy, discipline, obedience and inflexibility.*

It is left to one of Ho's compatriots, Tran Ngoc Danh, to offer perhaps the most succinct analysis of Ho's attitude:

> How many times in my life I've been asked: you who know Ho Chi Minh so well, can you say whether he is a nationalist or a communist? The answer is simple: Ho Chi Minh is both. For him, nationalism and communism, the end and the means, complement one another; or rather, they merge inextricably.[6]

The informed Marxist will either understand this quite well or dismiss it as impossible. Let us try to investigate the matter. We might begin with the young Cung arriving in London, where he meets one of his shipmates already a communist. He is probably taken along to a Party meeting and his imagination fired sufficiently to read the Communist Manifesto, with those opening words which for 123 years have never lost their unique and menacing pertinence:

> A spectre haunts Europe; the spectre of communism.

To discover Ho's next thoughts we need to remember that Marxism, unlike Confucianism, Buddhism or Christianity, has nothing to do with beliefs or ethics, but is in the nature of a scientific analysis. Marx shows the historic forces at work in society and how the ever-changing economic structure determines the pattern of social relationships. He postulates the inevitability, indeed the *infallibility*, of his analysis, in which the industrial working class is to be the instigator and the means of a new order that will necessarily emerge throughout the entire world. He shows, and considers that he has proved, how the pattern of change, of development, of conflict, will produce an inevitable clash between the capitalist 'haves' and the proletarian 'have-nots'. In the ensuing class-war (or revolution) the proletariat must inevitably come out on top since it forms the vast majority and needs only to unite to be all-powerful. Marx asserts that he does not *advocate* class-war (or revolution); he merely predicts it. But the reader cannot go far without sensing an incitement to rebellion. This is scarcely surprising: Marx was justifiably appalled by the effects of the industrial system as he saw it operating in England; and his revelation of its horrors in itself promotes the kind of indignation that sends youth scampering to the barricades.

---

[4] Quoted in *The Lost Revolution*, p. 48.   [5] *Sociologie d'une Guerre*.
[6] *Histoire du Président Ho*, Foreign Languages Press, Hanoi, 1949, p. 33.

Now what was there about Marx's analysis that appealed to Ho, an Asian divorced from Western ideologies and scarcely interested in the sufferings of the European industrial workers? First of all we should keep in mind that although Ho was something of a poet and a dreamer he was even more a practical person. He perceived that his fellow countrymen suffered economically, they were the 'have-nots' as against the French 'haves'; and Confucianism, Buddhism and Christianity offered them small comfort and no relief. Furthermore, the Vietnamese, like most orientals, were firm believers in Fate. The Marxist concept included the *inevitability* of proletarian victory. It is not without significance that the Vietnamese expression for revolution – *cach mang* – means literally 'change fate'.

Ho thus saw in Marxism a basic plan for revolutionary action. He was still a long way, of course, from turning this idea into detailed working-drawings. Some forty years later Ho himself explained how this came about in an article entitled 'The Path to Leninism', written for a Soviet publication.[7] Ho explains that in his early years in Paris he had joined the French Socialist Party, not because he understood their principles but because they had befriended him. Then had come the confusion about the various 'Internationals'. What Ho had wanted to know was: which International supported his own cause? Someone gave him Lenin's *Thesis on National and Colonial Questions*[8] which had been published in *l'Humanité*. For Ho this was the beacon light.

> There were political terms difficult to understand in this thesis. But by dint of reading it again and again, finally I could grasp the main part of it. What emotion, enthusiasm, clear-sightedness and confidence it instilled in me! . . . After that I had entire confidence in Lenin, in the Third International. At first, patriotism, not yet Communism led me to this. Step by step, by studying Marxism-Leninism parallel with participation in practical activities, I gradually became aware that only Socialism-Communism can liberate the oppressed nations and the working people of the world from slavery.[9]

The conditions of affiliation to the Communist International (the Comintern) included total acceptance of decisions from Moscow.

---

[7] Quoted fully in Ho Chi Minh, *Selected Works* (4 vols; Hanoi 1960–2), iv, pp. 448–50; or Lacouture *op. cit.*, pp. 21–3; or *Vietnam, History, Documents and Opinions*, pp. 37–9.

[8] In which Lenin made clear that Colonialism was merely the final stage of capitalism and was thus to be fought against in the coming world revolution. See V. I. Lenin, *Selected Works* (2 vols, Moscow 1952, ii, pp. 462–70).

[9] 'The path to Leninism'. In this brief statement regarding his political beliefs, Ho mentions in rapid sequence 'Communism', 'Marxism-Leninism', and 'Socialism-Communism', giving capitals to the first and third as well as to the second, thereby implying dogma rather than mere political concept. Either as dogma or concept these three terms can be variously interpreted. It would seem that Ho, writing for Soviet consumption at this particular time (1960), was anxious not to be too specific about the 'communism' he believed in. This was a period when he had to steer an intricate course between the rocks of Soviet and Chinese dogma. See pp. 115f.

Obedience to such decisions was implicit. Affiliated Parties furthermore had to agree to develop a systematic and persistent communist indoctrination within the trade unions, works committees, co-operatives, and other mass organizations of workers. Within such organizations it was necessary to set up cells, which, with unflagging zeal, had to win their members over to communism. The cells were to be completely subordinate to the Party as a whole.

It had been expected by Marx that the first communist revolution would take place in a highly developed industrialized country such as England or Germany. When events proved otherwise and the revolution came in agricultural Russia, Lenin found it necessary to devise a formula that would include the peasants, who were now to take an honoured place alongside the industrial proletariat. This, of course, became of great significance to a peasant country like Vietnam. Lenin's final contribution to Marxist theory (and for Ho his most important) was concerned with colonialism.[10] Perhaps because this final development of capitalism was largely post-Marx, it was left to Lenin to show how the populations of colonial countries were being exploited by the same capitalists that exploited the proletariat in the home country. The struggle for freedom was therefore a common cause. Lenin not only stated this common cause (superseding barriers of race, creed or colour), he also promised full support from the nation that had already achieved freedom, namely Soviet Russia.[11]

Before Ho read Marx or Lenin he understood only that the French had conquered his country and were keeping his compatriots in subjection. He saw that all efforts to combat French supremacy were ruthlessly put down and that every such uprising would fail unless a new method could be applied and outside help obtained. It was to seek such methods and such help that he had gone out into the world. Finding that there was no effective help either in America or England, he had turned to France, where he found friends amongst the socialists. They were ready to treat him as an equal, to teach him the theory of politics, how to write leaflets, how to publish propaganda sheets and how to hold meetings. But apart from offering sympathy, they were not really interested in Vietnamese affairs and had no intention of taking time and trouble on behalf of the Vietnamese people.

With the ending of the European war came Wilson and his Fourteen Points. But Ho discovered that the clause calling for self-determination of small nations proved a sham whenever it conflicted with the privileges of the Powers. Always the realist, even in his salad days, Ho saw that he had nothing to hope for there.

Meanwhile he had started reading Marx. Here he saw a pattern of social development that offered a key to his own aspirations. And later, when Lenin stated that Asiatic peasants and all such subject populations were, equally with Western workers, the victims of capitalism, the bell rang loud and clear. Every 'cause' needs a *logique*, a verbal framework, a unifying philosophy to serve as a *raison d'être*, a proselytizer, a guide,

10 V. I. Lenin, *op. cit.*

11 But whatever the sincerity of Lenin's intentions, his successors for the most part paid only lip-service to this promise, as Ho was very soon to discover (see p. 45).

and above all a dogma by which to exclude deviationist groups and concepts. Ho found this in Marxism-Leninism.[12]

At the Congress in Tours (1920), when he got up and made his impassioned speech, the Chairman responded with a polite declaration that 'the whole Socialist Party is with him in protesting against the crimes of the bourgeoisie'. But Ho wasn't interested in such platitudes. He soon discovered that amongst the Socialists there were some who were protesting in a vacuum (the Second International) and there were others, the Third International, who followed Lenin's call for action. For reasons already explained Ho voted with the latter. As one result of this he parted company with his friend Nguyen The Truyen (with whom he ran *Le Paria*) as well as with several other Vietnamese associates. 'While these continued to struggle for their country's independence,' comments Hoang Van Chi, 'Ho devoted himself to the cause of international communism.'[13] This particular interpretation shows with ironic clarity how men of understanding and integrity can form concepts totally opposed to those formed by other men of equal understanding and integrity[14] who might re-state this comment: 'While these continued to struggle fruitlessly for their country's independence Ho devoted himself to gaining it through international communism.'

It was inevitable from this time on that Ho would want to go to Moscow to study Leninism at source and if possible meet this avatar of the Marxist cosmos. But in the event, Lenin died (21 January 1924) before he got there or at least before a meeting was arranged. Everyone seems to differ as to the exact date of Ho's arrival in Moscow. Possibly he went there twice in 1923. This is indeed stated as a fact by Hoang Van Chi, who also offers us an interesting comment as to means of travel: 'To get to Moscow, Vietnamese communists used to buy, at low cost, a Kuomintang passport from the Chinese Embassy in Paris. They pretended to be Chinese citizens wanting to go back to China by way of Moscow and Vladivostok.'[15]

The Japanese writer, Kyo Komatsu, who was living in Paris at that

---

[12] Perhaps the best exposition of Ho's inevitable utilization of Marxism-Leninism will be found in the biography written by Truong Chinh, *President Ho Chi Minh, Revered Leader of the Vietnamese People*, Foreign Languages Press, Hanoi, 1966. As the title suggests, this work is limited by its partisanship: the author being a strong Maoist, Lacouture (*op. cit.*, p. 189) suggests that he cannot help treating his own leader with the veneration the Chinese Leader is accorded. Be that as it may, the political insight is often revealing, as for example (Truong Chinh, *op. cit.*, p. 49): President Ho was the first leader of the Vietnamese revolution to discern the misguidedness of the methods – isolated assassinations, mutinies – employed by his predecessors, who relied on adventuristic acts of individual heroism. He was convinced that if the revolution was to triumph, action must be taken to rouse the political consciousness of the masses, to organize them, to draw them into the struggle for commonplace demands.

[13] *From Colonialism to Communism*, p. 39.

[14] Such as Bernard Fall, Marvin Gettleman, Ellen Hammer and Jean Chesneaux: see Bibliography.

[15] *ibid.*, p. 40.

time and knew Ho well, says that the Vietnamese leader wanted him to come along on a trip he made in November 1923. Komatsu turned down the offer so Ho went alone.[16] He seems to have made the same quiet impact on Moscow that he made on Paris. Lacouture quotes Ruth Fischer (a significant intellectual in the German Communist Party) as saying that when he first arrived he seemed very inconsequential. Nevertheless:

> He struck a delightful note of goodness and simplicity. . . . Also his temperament inclined him far more towards action and putting ideas into effect than towards doctrinal debates. . . . He played a big part in things, bigger than some of the better-known Asian leaders of the time: Mao did not come to the fore until later.[17]

This is a point often overlooked: that long before Mao, Stalin, Gandhi or Nehru were heard of outside their own orbit, Ho had become known to a wide European circle, which was soon to be extended by contacts all over the Far East.

In Moscow, Ho was, indeed, soon on easy terms with all the top revolutionaries: Trotsky, Dimitrov, Radek, Bukharin and particularly Stalin, who, when he had been People's Commissar of Nationality Affairs, had made a special study of colonial problems. He was to outlive all these Old Guard revolutionaries, and in many respects to outshine them: Trotsky was more brilliant intellectually and a more outstanding theoretician; but practically he accomplished less. Stalin inherited an empire already forged by Lenin and could scarcely be said to have improved it.

In the summer of 1924 Ho was already making his mark at the Fifth Congress of the Communist International. He began by taking to task not only the 'reformist' group of the Second International but even the whole French Communist Party, whom he accused of ignoring colonial problems:

> It's the duty of our communist press to familiarize our militants with colonial problems, to wake up the struggling masses in the colonies and to gain their support on behalf of communism. What have we done in this respect? Absolutely nothing. If we compare the space given in *l'Humanité*, the central organ of our Party, with that given to the same topic by the bourgeois Press such as *Le Temps*, *le Figaro*, *l'Œuvre*, or the less rigid papers such as *Le Populaire* and *La Liberté*, we see at once that the comparison is scarcely in our favour.

Having quoted statistics showing the overwhelming size and population of the colonial dependencies as compared with the occupying powers, he reminded his audience of Lenin's thesis: that the success of the revolution in Western Europe was closely tied to national aspirations in the colonies and enslaved countries of the East; that this movement was, indeed, part of the general proletarian revolution. After citing repeated examples of *l'Humanité*'s failure to deal with colonial problems Ho politely exposed the inadequacy of the proposals put forward by

[16] Lacouture, *Ho Chi Minh*, p. 32.   [17] *ibid.*, p. 32.

the Soviet delegate, Manuilsky, thus bearding the lion in his own den. According to a Soviet source[18] Ho even protested to Zinoviev, at that time perhaps Stalin's number-two man, about Soviet neglect. The inference is that Ho was by no means satisfied with the Comintern's Eurocentric approach to revolution, which largely ignored Lenin's thesis. Perhaps Ho was already beginning to doubt Lenin's real intention or ability to implement this thesis, which the Russian leader had put forward largely to counter the demands of M. N. Roy, at that period a powerful Indian communist exponent. Ho ended his speech with a specific five-point programme:

1 Regular weekly space in *l'Humanité* on colonial affairs.
2 Expanded propaganda in the colonies; recruitment of new members and formation of cells.
3 Colonial comrades to be sent to the University for Oriental Workers in Moscow.
4 The French trade union executive to organize the colonial workers then in France.
5 All Party members to take a more active role in colonial affairs.

We see here a very different Ho from that emotional young man at the Tours Congress. He now seems able to deal with political problems on an international scale and on level terms with the hierarchy of the communist world. One has only to glance at his five points to see why it was necessary for him to link up with international communism. Successful revolutions, like successful business enterprises, need not only long and careful preparation but also the help and guidance of experts. From this time on Ho tied his cause to world communism, which at all times (at least until recently) was directed from Moscow. The question may be asked: did these two interests never conflict? It would appear that by and large they seldom did. It usually suited Soviet policy to promote, or at least to encourage, national insurrection. As for Ho himself: to be loyal to international communism at every point in his career may not entirely have suited his policy; but he seems to have realized that obedience and Party discipline were inherent in the overall objective.

On this particular visit (1924) Ho spent up to a year in Russia, a large part of the time in the University of Oriental Workers, where he learned amongst other things that while Marx evolved a theory, Lenin showed how to turn that theory into practice. Marx had said 'Revolution is an art'. Lenin worked out the technique of that art, which may be briefly stated:

1 A revolution must never be started until the insurgents are ready to fight to victory.
2 The leaders must choose the right place, i.e. where they have conditions most favourable to them and forces superior to the *status quo*.
3 Leaders must choose the right time: essentially when government forces are weak, demoralized, scattered, unready.

[18] *Inprecor*, 17 July 1924. See McLane, *op. cit.*, p. 37.

4 Superiority of morale being a *sine qua non*, propaganda must always be invigorating.
5 Offensive being another *sine qua non*, to be on the defensive is to invite defeat.

Echoing Danton's rallying cry, *De l'audace, et encore de l'audace, et toujours de l'audace*, Lenin emphasized that hesitation, weakness, pity, deviation, reformism and compromise all helped the enemy. Remembering the goal, the communist could not shirk the means. Violence wins the revolution; dictatorship consolidates it. Both require ruthless leadership.

This was the gospel Ho took away from Moscow. He followed it closely but not to the letter. He devised his own gospel. It is contained in this phrase: The ability to perceive what is feasible at one point in history and what is not. Although Lenin also had this ability Ho added something special: the ability to consider the limitations as well as the capacities of the human beings involved.

There is something else in Ho's character that one does not find in any other top political figure, not even (to mention two considered more humane) Gandhi and Nehru. This is what Confucius called '*shu*'. There is no exact equivalent in English; the nearest we might get is 'reciprocity' in the sense of those responses between two human beings aware of the concept that all men are brothers. Ho's instinct seems to have been to work from the heart rather than from the head. 'To see something, to feel something and then to interpret one's impressions; to try and distinguish between the appearance and reality of things; that's all. What's so difficult about it?'[19] By calling for a response in people's hearts Ho seems to have won not only the affection of his own people but a vibration in the hearts of thousands of young Americans, who were ready to believe that, no matter how savage the conflict, his humanity never declared war on their humanity.

As Bernard Fall puts it: 'Ho was always intimate, always accessible, always truly uncle. Compare this to the remoteness and austerity of Mao or even Chou.'[20] Ho could say that he hated the French and mean it, but this was a hatred of what certain Frenchmen had done to his family, his friends, or his countrymen. There is seldom if ever an instance when he translated this impersonal animosity into specific hatred of one individual. A person whom he had reason to hate, Louis Arnoux, chief of the Indo-China Secret Police, who opposed and even hounded him for twenty years, is able 'to speak of him with liking and respect'[21] – a feeling that could scarcely have been inspired by any hate on Ho's part. And consider this tribute from Hoang Van Chi, made at a time when this writer had already become an opponent of Ho's régime:

In addition to his remarkable intelligence, Ho is endowed with an outstanding personality. He has in fact all the qualities necessary in

---

[19] Tran Ngoc Danh, quoting Ho in *Histoire du Président Ho*, Foreign Languages Press, Hanoi, 1949, p. 33.
[20] *The Two Vietnams*, Frederick A. Praeger, N.Y. 1964, p. 82.
[21] Lacouture, *op. cit.*, p. 16.

a leader, and his austerity, perseverance, iron determination and whole hearted devotion to the cause of Revolution are an inspiration to all who serve under him and to the nation as a whole.[22]

In view of Ho's character and accomplishments, it seems curious that, although we have Marxism, Leninism, Stalinism, and Titoism, we have no Hoism. When at one point late in his life he became a cult, it was largely among youth that the hosannas were shouted; and youth is fickle in its loyalties. Perhaps Ho does not go with 'isms'. What he represents is less a political cult than a philosophical concept. For want of a better word let us call his contribution Hochiminity.

[22] *From Colonialism to Communism*, p. 33.

5 Agent

You are only a very ordinary cock,
But every morning you crow to announce the dawn
Cock-a-doodle-do! You rouse the people from sleep.
Truly your daily job is not unimportant.

In January 1925 it was felt by the Comintern that Ho had learned enough of communist technique to be sent out into the field. Under the pseudonym of Vuong, he was therefore attached to the Borodin mission then being despatched to China, the background of which was as follows: The 19th century had been a period of continual humiliation for China. In pursuit of trade, the encroaching West had forced a reluctant self-contained China to open up first its ports then its hinterland. Pursuing the arts of peace and neglecting defence, China was unable to resist Western gunboats and artillery, and forced to sign increasingly harsh treaties. The blame for these humiliations fell on the ruling Manchus (invaders from the north-east who had conquered China in the 17th century); a fertile bed of revolt was thus prepared. Amongst the insurrectionists was Sun Yat-sen, a Western-educated doctor. In 1911, when the revolt broke out, Sun was nominated first President of the Republic of China. But since he and his party, the Kuomintang,[1] were then considered too far left by many of the contending Chinese war lords, he never achieved real control, and died in 1925 before seeing unification become effective. Foremost amongst his lieutenants was Chiang Kai-shek, then a young army officer.

Meanwhile, the Soviets had seen in this revolt the seeds of the next communist revolution. Having recognized Sun's weakness in his lack of military strength, it had been decided to despatch a military mission that would help him combat the troublesome war lords. Kuomintang strength was centred in the south, and particularly in Canton – traditionally a rebel area, and with a pro-rebel military academy at Whampoa. It was therefore to Canton that, despite Sun's sudden death, the mission proceeded, led by Soviet military expert Mikhail Borodin.

Ho was chosen to accompany Borodin for various reasons: first, because he was something of an expert on Far-eastern affairs; second, because he spoke Cantonese; third, and perhaps most important, because he could organize the considerable population of Vietnamese in South China. Most of these were political dissidents who had been attracted to this revolutionary area not only because of its generally leftist reputation but because of a recent *coup de théâtre*: Pham Hong Thai, a member of the revolutionary group called Tam Tam Xa, had thrown a bomb at the car of the Indo-China Governor-General, M. Merlin. Although this hadn't succeeded in killing him it had produced enough *réclame* to establish Canton as an exciting revolutionary mecca, both for political dissidents and students. It was amongst

[1] Three Chinese characters *Kuo Min Tang* (KMT) meaning Nationalist Party.

these students, not yet indoctrinated with divergent and therefore 'false' dogma, that Ho found his best material. One such eager young man was Pham Van Dong. The son of a mandarin at the court of Hué, he had given up the fleshpots for the life of a rebel and had recently helped to stage a rising in Hanoi. Escaping to Canton, he was then trained by Ho in the art of revolution. Dong later went back to Vietnam to set up cells, emerging twenty years afterwards as Ho's Prime Minister.

In addition to training students, Ho (using his pseudonym, Vuong) formed the Vietnam Revolutionary Youth League (Thanh Nien). With the use of 'jelly'-type transfers he produced a propaganda news sheet. There were also regular classes in socialist doctrine and methods. One of the pupils, Le Manh Trinh, who, along with several compatriots, had made the long and arduous journey from Saigon as a ship's stowaway specifically to join Ho's group, describes what he found on arrival in Canton:

> Our curriculum consisted of various subjects: the history of the evolution of humanity, especially from the beginning of capitalism to imperialism; the history of the liberation movement in Korea, China, India and the history of Vietnam under foreign domination; theories such as Gandhi-ism and Sun Yat-sen's doctrine; Marxism-Leninism together with the history of the October revolution; the history and organization of the three internationals, the international organization of women, youths and peasants, the Red International Relief Association, the Peasants' International, etc. We also learned how to carry out propaganda and to set up a network of organization for workers, farmers, youths, students, etc. A chart of organizations showed the many sections, branches and affiliations. At special classes some of us played the part of propagandists, others pretended to be workers, farmers or students listening and putting questions. Afterwards we made observations and criticisms. Each reported in turn what he had grasped from the lectures; while the others listened and corrected the incorrect statements. We also wrote for the class news-bulletin. Criticism and self-criticism meetings were held regularly. Vuong always explained things in a simple way so that everybody could understand, and remembered statistics very well. Saying that we should always pay attention to the value of statistics he quoted Lenin: 'Farmers believe more in facts and figures than in theories.'[2]

Le Man Trinh describes this 'Vuong' as 'rather tall and thin, with a broad forehead, bright eyes, a sweet and warm voice; he was joyful but seldom laughed; he always wore a Sun Yat-sen type of suit'.[3]

Another of the students trained in this school was Nguyen Luong Bang, a sailor on a French warship. Fired with revolutionary zeal by the news of the bomb attack on hated Governor-General Merlin, he utilized his next arrival in the port of Canton to meet the already well-known leader of the Thanh Tien (Revolutionary Youth) group:

[2] *Days with Ho Chi Minh*, pp. 107/9.
[3] This is a buttoned-to-the-neck dark jacket and trousers.

Mr Vuong arranged to meet me in front of a big department store in
Canton. When I arrived for the appointment on that winter's day he
was already there. He was still quite young, about 35; thin but strong,
with very bright eyes. He inquired about my age, my work and about
the conditions of the Vietnamese sailors working on the French
warships. I felt that not only was he a true patriot but like an elder
brother who wanted to take care of me.

Apart from training us in politics, Mr Vuong taught us general
education including the English language. He did not miss any
occasion to educate us and set us right. Once, when we spoke off-
handedly about the sailors he gently reproved us: 'Why do you speak
of them like that? They are our brothers.'[4]

After receiving his training, Bang was ready to go back to Vietnam to
start indoctrinating. Vuong's final advice: 'Since you come from abroad
the security agents will be on your tail. So for the first few days, be
careful where you go. Don't call in anywhere. If necessary put the police
off the scent by pretending to be a bad lot.'[5]

During the same period Ho, with Borodin's help, was also sending
his compatriots to the Whampoa military academy. His future adherents
thus gained military as well as political training. At this academy
Borodin had as associates both Chou En-lai and Chiang Kai-shek. Sun
Yat-sen having died, Chiang began to take his place as the main
protagonist of the New China, and used Sun's name with a diplomatic
awareness of its continuing prestige. He was also astute in combining his
own military strength with that other requirement for a dictator: money.
Chiang got this by leaguing with the bankers, especially the enormously
powerful Soong family, one of whose daughters he had married.

Ho got to know both Chou and Chiang. With the former he was
always friendly: Ho and Chou En-lai, indeed, had much in common:
determination, sincerity, humanity and an international approach,
including knowledge of languages. With Chiang, on the other hand,
Ho was always at a distance. The distrust was mutual: they worked
towards opposite goals. In 1927, when Chiang felt himself well in the
saddle, he turned on his pro-communist associates, imprisoning and
even executing many. Appropriating the political machinery of the
Kuomintang and taking a leaf out of Mussolini's book, he turned a
socialist party into a military autocracy. Thanh Nien, Ho's school and
the entire Vietnamese revolutionary group in Canton were all pounced
upon. Borodin himself anticipated the coup and warned his associates
as best he could. Ho escaped on a boat to Vladivostok and so via the
Trans-Siberian railway to Moscow, where he arrived early in 1928. On
this occasion the records of his activities there are slight. No doubt,
having returned from a difficult and dangerous assignment, he was

---

[4] *Days with Ho Chi Minh*, pp. 62/3.
[5] According to P. J. Honey (quoted in *Time*, 12 September 1971), it was at
this time (1925) that Ho is supposed to have 'betrayed a rival nationalist
leader, who was seized by the French and executed in Hanoi'. In extenuation
for this act of treachery 'he offered three justifications': a dangerous rival
was eliminated; the execution stirred up anti-French feeling; Ho's blood-
money went to augment Party funds. No source for this is given.

now accepted as one of the élite amongst the non-Russian communists. We see some evidence of this in his being sent, that same year, to the Congress against Imperialist War, first in Brussels (where Madame Sun Yat-sen and Nehru both attended); then to similar conferences in France, Germany, Switzerland and Italy. Clearly Ho, as a practical and experienced Party member, was now something of a show-piece.

There was, however, a more practical assignment awaiting him. In Bangkok, a South Asiatic Bureau of the Comintern had been set up under a French communist, Hilaire Noulens. Because of Chiang's coup in China, Bangkok had become the new Canton for Vietnamese dissidents. Meanwhile, thousands of others had, over the years, been journeying overland via Laos to seek refuge in Siam's north-east – a remote and largely forbidding tract of jungle and mountains. Ho's mission was to contact, organize and instruct these potential recruits.

His first concern, as usual, was to learn the language. Thus he added Siamese to his already extensive repertoire. To elude agents of the French *Sûreté* operating in the area he took a new pseudonym, Thau Chin, and proceeded cautiously up country to Phichit in central Siam. This was a fairly comfortable railway journey. But his main target was Udon, up towards the Laos border, where there were several thousands of his compatriots. Amongst those he met in Phichit was Le Manh Trinh, whom we have already encountered as one of 'Vuong's' pupils in Canton and who had subsequently been sent into Siam to form cells. Le Manh Trinh tells us:

> In Phichit the number of Vietnamese was small, their organization fairly good, but it was rather closely watched by the secret police. Mr Chin [Ho] stayed there for only ten days. Then he went with us to Udon, about ten days' walk from Phichit through the forests. Each of us had to carry two boxes of clothes, a cutlass, a bamboo tube full of salted chicken or pork and ten kilos of rice. Seeing that Mr Chin was not accustomed to carrying things on shoulder-poles we offered to take his boxes, but he refused. After two or three days, we found that his feet were swollen and bleeding. But he smiled, saying they would soon get used to it. Indeed, after the fourth day, Mr Chin was able to follow the rest of us quite well.[6]

In Udon, Ho opened a school, published a news-sheet and founded a peasant co-operative. Returning to Bangkok for similar activities he made a surprising change from communism to Buddhism; or, rather, he enlisted the sympathies of the bonzes by showing the relationship between the two concepts as expounded by Engels.[7] Himself donning

---

[6] *Days with Ho Chi Minh*, pp. 112/13.

[7] For an interesting exposition of the relationship between Marxism and Buddhism see the chapter on 'Dialectical Materialism' by Professor R. C. Zaehner in *The Concise Encyclopedia of Living Faiths*, Hutchinson 1971, and particularly his commentary on Engels, for example: 'Marxism does not consider itself to be a religion, but in his later works, particularly *Anti-Dühring* and *The Dialectics of Nature*, Engels does in fact deal with what are usually considered to be specifically religious issues . . . in his and Marx's analysis of matter he is at one with Buddhism.'

the yellow robe, he set up cells inside the monasteries and subtly preached the gospel of St Marx. These seeds of communist thought may have helped to produce that later harvest of Buddhist uprisings against the Ngo Dinh Diem régime.

While Ho was busy on these Siamese projects, the Thanh Nien (Revolutionary Youth) movement earlier founded in Canton had slowly re-emerged from Chiang Kai-shek's persecutions and had seeded itself in various centres of concentrated industry, such as Saigon, Hanoi, Haiphong, Shanghai and Hong Kong. Because of growing labour unrest and consequent support from the workers, the political groups so formed had been able to move more openly into declared communist doctrine. But because Ho was no longer present to exercise his special flair for containing factionalism, at least three divergent bodies had emerged: the Indo-Chinese Communist Party, the Anna-mese Communist Party, and the Indo-China Communist League. This divergence had of course resulted in weaker discipline and security; and in Indo-China particularly the authorities were able to make wholesale arrests. Towards the end of 1929 the Comintern, alarmed at this disruption, detached Ho from his Bangkok assignment and sent him off to Hong Kong, where the fractured militants for the most part maintained headquarters. They would appear to have already become uneasy at the disabling effects of their split and willing enough to respond to Ho's call for unity. At the subsequent meeting (said to have taken place amidst the hurly-burly of a Hong Kong football match)[8] Ho persuaded them to amalgamate into a single Communist Party in 1930. At first it was called the Vietnamese Communist Party, but this was soon expanded to become the Indo-Chinese Communist Party (ICP), in order to include Laos and Cambodia. Headquarters were established in Hanoi and the following aims formulated:[9]

1 Overthrow French imperialism, feudalism, and the reactionary Vietnamese capitalists.
2 Establish complete independence of Indo-China.
3 Form a government of workers, peasants and soldiers.
4 Confiscate the banks and other imperialist enterprises.
5 Confiscate plantations and other estates and redistribute them amongst the peasants.
6 Introduce an eight-hour working day.
7 Abolish forced loans, poll-tax and all taxes bearing heavily upon the poor.
8 Establish democratic liberty.
9 Provide universal education.
10 Establish equality between men and women.

This programme, more or less the straight Party line, seems violently revolutionary in comparison with Ho's Eight Points put forward for the Versailles Conference only a decade earlier. From being a youth still green in political theory and totally inexperienced in political action he had in these ten years become the most significant agent of the

---

[8] Lacouture, *op. cit.*, p. 43.
[9] See *Vietnam, History, Documents and Opinions*, pp. 40/42.

Comintern in South East Asia; and was, indeed, shortly to be appointed head of its Far Eastern Bureau.

There was one revolutionary party that had stayed outside Ho's amalgamation: the Vietnamese Nationalist Party, usually referred to as the VNQDD (Viet Nam Quoc Dan Dang). Taking its inspiration from the Chinese Kuomintang (KMT), its aim was to overthrow French rule by revolution and then establish a 'republican' government along KMT lines. It was the VNQDD that in this same February 1930 (when Ho formed the ICP) inspired and led the revolt of the Vietnamese garrison troops at Yen Bay on the Tonkin-China border. This had been intended as the first move in a series of revolts that would explode into the proposed 'revolution'. But because of VNQDD bungling the French got wind of the affair and put down the rising with the usual severity. Despite active help from the Chinese Kuomintang, the VNQDD never properly recovered from the Yen Bay disaster.

This failure of the only rival greatly strengthened Ho's new ICP grouping; and within a year its membership had grown from an original 200 to well over a thousand.[10] But outside the Party members there were tens of thousands of adherents affiliated to the workers' syndicates; and even larger numbers in the peasant organizations. At this period (1931) all these have-nots were potential rebels. The Great Depression spreading outwards from America had disrupted trade, provoked wide unemployment and sent prices downwards in a disastrous spiral.[11] Worst hit were the industrial workers who lost their jobs. Since there was neither insurance nor 'relief' they and their families were left to beg, steal or starve. As it happened, in Vietnam the proportion of such unemployed was small, because the French industrialists were for some time able to undercut the falling world prices by wage reductions. Despite such wage cuts those workers still employed found themselves almost as well off as before, since the depressed prices of commodities enabled them to buy food and other basics at ever-lower prices. It was the peasant population that really suffered. Under French pressure vast areas of land had been given over to rice and rubber, both of which were driven to almost impossible depths by constant short selling on world markets. Furthermore, a succession of crop failures inside Indo-China, which might normally have strengthened prices, had no effect on the world market, and for the Indo-China peasant merely added famine to the prevailing economic ruin.

Out of such miseries is revolution born. Singularly enough, it was in Nghe An province, Ho's birthplace, and traditionally also the birthplace of revolt, that the first outburst came. Largely thanks to the permeations of the ICP the natives were not only seething to rebel but organized to make rebellion thrive. Six thousand peasants assembled to form a vast hunger march to Vinh. Big estates were seized and redistributed amongst the starving populace. In many villages people's councils were set up under the name of 'Xo-Viets', which thus established both

---

[10] See *Vietnam, History, Documents and Opinions*, p. 34.

[11] In our prevailing inflationary epoch we think of *rising* prices as a threat, largely forgetting that inflation goes with affluence. Deflation, on the other hand, goes with depression, and during such periods the whole population suffers except those lucky ones who sell short.

their nature and their nationality. Peasant demonstrations elsewhere were backed by strikes in the factories. It was the largest and most effective revolt in Vietnamese history to date. Nevertheless, it did not take into account those five precepts of Lenin's; and especially the first one: *Revolution must never be started until you are ready to fight to victory.* When the French Foreign Legion turned machine-guns on the marching throngs they proved the accuracy of a different precept, *jus est in armis.*[12]

Following this slaughter, wholesale arrests were made not only amongst the demonstrators but amongst the ICP, whose thousand-strong members in Nghe An and Ha Tinh were considered to have engineered the uprisings. Whether or not they actually did has never been established: on the one hand it could be considered a powerful demonstration of ICP strength; on the other hand, it would not have been in line with Ho's usual caution about premature rebellion. Nevertheless his programme for the ICP addressed to 'workers, peasants, soldiers, young people and students' had called for the overthrow of French Imperialism; and within a few months this was followed by an insurrection on the part of those same workers, peasants, soldiers, young people and students. The result was that, although the ICP came out of this affair with increased psychological strength, they were greatly weakened in organizational capacity, having lost by execution or imprisonment many of their top men. Pham Van Dong was amongst those captured. He was sent to Poulo Condore, where he would certainly have perished had the French Popular Front government of six years later not granted a general amnesty.

After the successful launching of the ICP in Hong Kong, Ho had gone to Shanghai,[13] where several thousand Vietnamese militiamen were on duty in the French Settlement. One of Ho's former pupils in Canton, Nguyen Luong Bang (whom we took leave of when he returned to Vietnam to set up cells), had already started organizational work amongst these compatriots. One evening early in 1930 he received a note 'worded like a love letter. "I will be waiting for you in the billiard room of the Hsien Shil Company (a big department store)." I guessed that it had been sent by one of our comrades.'[14]

Bang keeps the suggested appointment but no one is there. Upon going out of the store, however, he hears a whisper behind him and recognizes 'Vuong'. They arrange to meet the next morning at Vuong's 'hotel'.

His room, rented at a cheap price, was only large enough for a single bed and a small table. There was no stove and it was very cold. On the table I saw plenty of books – mostly in English and Chinese – and some typewriters, all with English keyboards. 'You must be very cautious in your work amongst the Vietnamese soldiers' he told me. 'They are very enthusiastic; but, with arms in their hands, they are prone to reckless action.' A few days later, we heard of the Yen Bay

[12] Might makes right. Seneca.
[13] According to Charles B. McLane, *op. cit.*, p. 135, Ho was also said to have been the Comintern representative in Singapore at this time (1930).
[14] *Days with Ho Chi Minh*, p. 67.

uprising and its failure. We realized all the more keenly the significance of Vuong's teaching.

At another meeting he told us: 'The revolutionary movement is
growing everywhere. There's so much to do and our means are
limited. To handle it all, we need help from the local Communist
Party. In whatever country we work in, we need to be guided by
them.[15]

Later on, the writer adds, he was to discover how helpful the Chinese
Communist Party could be:

Our work consisted of writing articles for *The Bugler*. The printing
and distribution of this paper to the barracks in which the Vietnamese soldiers were stationed was handled by our Chinese comrades.
They also supplied us with files, stencil paper and steel-nibbed
pens for mimeographing. This was the first time we co-operated
with a fraternal Party. From then on we realized the meaning of
communist internationalism which we had formerly known in theory
only.[16]

In July or August 1930, Vuong came to Shanghai again. He
attended a meeting in our office and made many suggestions about
agitation among the Vietnamese soldiers. 'We must arouse their
homesickness, then their love for their home country and their
compatriots. Only in such a way can we go deep into people's
hearts.' Vuong ran over some issues of *The Bugler*, and reminded
us that we should not use difficult words, but should write short,
concise, and clear sentences. He then wrote some articles, in prose
as well as in verse, dealing with patriotism and the hatred for French
domination. These articles were worded in very terse and simple
language.[17]

Soon after this Bang was informed upon and picked up by the French
Sûreté.

They beat me until I fainted. When I came to they showed me a
photograph. 'Do you know this man, Nguyen Ai Quoc, your leader?
He's been arrested in Hongkong. If you've got any sense, you'll talk.'
I looked at the portrait. So Vuong was Nguyen Ai Quoc![18]

In 1931 we find Ho returning to Hong Kong under a new pseudonym,
Tong Van So. The French had already sentenced to death Nguyen Ai
Quoc, alias this and alias that, and were clamouring for his extradition.
Two other Comintern agents were in Hong Kong at this time, Hilaire
Noulens (with whom Ho had worked in Siam five years earlier) and
Joseph Ducroux, who describes the Ho he then met, aged forty-one:

---

[15] *ibid.*, p. 68.
[16] This is a neat demonstration of why Ho had chosen to work within the
international movement.
[17] *Days with Ho Chi Minh*, p. 70.
[18] *ibid.*, p. 72. Bang spent eight years in gaol before he managed to escape. It
was August 1945 before they met again.

I've seldom met a human being who lived so frugally and was so disdainful of every comfort. The energy he showed! He was taut and quivering. He had only one thought in his head – and it has, I think, obsessed him all his life long. His country, Vietnam. I won't say he wasn't a sincere internationalist, a true revolutionary. But to him, Vietnam had always come first.[19]

'It's surprising', comments Bernard Fall,[20] 'that a personality like Ho has never caught the attention of a writer of thrillers or a producer of adventure films; his story combines all the necessary elements: conspirator and statesman, subtle scholar and political agitator of the first order.' Suddenly the British decided to clean up political troublemakers, with whom Hong Kong is periodically infested. In the general sweep, the two Frenchmen and Ho were all arrested.[21] Either Ho's pseudonym covered his true identity or the Colonial government decided not to reveal it to the French. He was given the comparatively light sentence of six months. It happened that even so they overplayed their hand. A barrister named Frank Loseby who had met Ho and (inevitably!) liked him, used a writ of habeas corpus to require proper charges to be made. The Colonial government produced 'conspiring to overthrow', etc. When Loseby appealed, Sir Stafford Cripps, then Solicitor-General, threw out the charges as having no basis under British law.[22] Ho was therefore released. It had also been realized by a British doctor that Ho had tuberculosis of the lungs. This doctor offered to get him into a sanatorium in England. Half anxious, half reluctant, Ho agreed to go for treatment and was put aboard a ship sailing for England. The Hong Kong Special Branch suspected he had slipped out of their hands for purposes they considered nefarious. When the ship called at Singapore Ho was picked up and brought back. Special Branch now had a valid charge: violating the immigration rules by leaving the Colony without the necessary documents. Given another term of imprisonment, Ho was transferred to the prison hospital. After several months rest and treatment, during which he endeared himself to the hospital staff, it was not too difficult for another of· Ho's friends to arrange his 'escape'. As a cover-up for the staff it was given out that he had died.[23]

---

[19] Lacouture, *op. cit.*, p. 48.

[20] *Le Viet Minh*, p. 20.

[21] According to Charles B. McLane (*op. cit.*, p. 147), it was Ducroix's prior arrest that led to the exposure of the other two.

[22] A splendid instance of *fiat justicia*, although one suspects a less left-wing Solicitor-General would have interpreted British law more conveniently for Hong Kong officialdom.

[23] This is the story that was given me in 1946 by an official of the Hong Kong government who had been present in the Colony when these events took place. It differs in some small detail from other accounts. For instance, Bernard Fall, *op. cit.*, p. 31, has Ho's escape from the prison hospital the result of an arrangement whereby he was to work for British Intelligence, and suggests that this accords with Ho's later arrangement to work for American Intelligence. But as we shall see, Ho's association with the Americans was strictly the result of events connected with World War II.

Smuggled on to the first outgoing coastal vessel, Ho slipped ashore at Amoy, where he set up temporarily as a Chinese merchant. Dead or alive, he was now, thanks to Chiang, the French *Sûreté* and British Special Branch, a strictly wanted man throughout China, Indo-China and British possessions. It was therefore essential that he should disappear until his death was fully accepted. The date was then autumn 1932. Ho stayed on in Amoy until spring of the following year.[24]

Meanwhile, the death of Nguyen Ai Quoc had been reported in *l'Humanité* as well as the Soviet Press. Finally his file at the French *Sûreté* was closed with the notation: 'Died in the Hongkong gaol'. Thus it was that Nguyen Ai Quoc became officially dead.

[24] This was one of several periods when Ho was supposed to have taken a wife. See Bernard Fall, *op. cit.*, p. 32. And Hoang Van Chi, for instance, states (*op. cit.*, p. 35): 'According to reliable sources Ho took a Chinese wife in Hong Kong and had a daughter by her. The same sources disclosed that in 1949 he asked the Chinese Communist Party to make inquiries as to her whereabouts, but no trace of the woman could be found.' This writer also states (*op. cit.*, p. 52) that one of Ho's associates in Moscow, Nguyen Khanh Toan, had a visit from a woman who claimed that she had been appointed Ho's wife during his stay in Soviet Russia. This writer does not designate his 'reliable sources' and his reports sound dubious.

6 Traveller

Nine days of ceaseless rain for one day of fine weather!
Really the sky above must be a pitiless thing.
My shoes are in pieces, the muddy road soils my feet,
But however it is done I have to keep on moving.

In April of that year (1933), with Ho's death established, the Comintern apparently decided it was safe for him to travel, and he was directed to return to Moscow for a fresh assignment. To get there he needed funds as well as active assistance of the Chinese Communist Party. This meant going to Shanghai, where, following numerous left-wing insurrections, Chiang Kai-shek's secret police were picking up all suspects.

Arriving in Shanghai, Ho seems to have borrowed a line from Shakespeare: 'Boldness, be my friend! Arm me audacity from head to foot!' Acquiring a smartish suit and hiring a limousine to go with it he had the chauffeur drive him to Madame Sun Yat-sen's house. She was the one leftist in Shanghai whose prestige was such that Chiang's secret police didn't dare harm her. Nevertheless, they took the precaution of ringing her house with plain-clothes men, so that characters like Ho couldn't make contact. Ho's suit and limousine deceived them into letting him through. Not to risk a conversation that the servants might report he merely left a letter. Madame Sun put him secretly in touch with Vaillant-Couturier, who happened to be in Shanghai; and it was through the Frenchman that Ho finally got from the Chinese Communist Party his travel ticket to Moscow.[1]

The route was again via Vladivostok and the Trans-Siberian railway. Ho arrived in Moscow some time in 1934. According to Bang he attended courses at the Lenin school prior to participating the following year in the Seventh Congress of the Communist International. This period was a nightmare in Soviet history. Apart from repeated crop failures plaguing the peasants the widespread purges meant that nobody could go secure of life and limb; Stalin's rigidity against instigating a common front had helped Hitler's rise to power; Japan having conquered Manchuria was on the Siberian doorstep; and the world depression had penetrated even Russia's economic walls.

There is no record of how Ho succeeded in threading a path through this entanglement of misery, hate, suspicion, accusation and sudden death. No doubt while at the Lenin school he could feel himself divorced from practical politics. At the Seventh Congress of the International, however, every delegate was called upon to make decisions that might easily displease the hierarchy. One dangerous dilemma concerned the tactics now required to confront rising fascism. Because Stalin had so far vetoed co-operation with any left-wing groups not totally controlled by the Comintern, Hitler had been able to knock down such groups one by one, including the German Communist Party

[1] *Days with Ho Chi Minh*, p. 81.

itself. Clearly the only hope of holding the fascist tide elsewhere in Europe was to organize any remaining elements that could be considered anti-fascist (or at least non-fascist) into a single co-operative front – the so-called Popular Front of later years. At the Congress Ho was one of two delegates who urged such a course. Fortunately for him the other was Dimitrov, whose prestige then could scarcely be challenged, even by Stalin. When the vote was taken, the majority of the delegates came out in favour of a united front.

Meanwhile a different sort of political football match was taking place in Macao (the Portuguese colony in South China), where the Indo-Chinese Communist Party was holding its first Party Congress. Operating without Ho's guidance, the Party members voted for a policy of continued rigid militancy in line with the Third International, i.e. excluding co-operation with other left-wing groups. According to Bernard Fall,[2] Ho hurried off (if such a term can be applied to a journey that occupied several weeks) to acquaint them with the new Popular Front policy.[3] Already in 1936 we find the ICP distinguishing between those French colonialists still to be considered the enemy and those who were considered 'anti-fascist' and therefore worthy to join the new club. For the ICP this turnabout became more acceptable when Léon Blum's Popular Front government in France (openly supported by the French Communist Party) granted legality to the ICP. Many political prisoners, including Pham Van Dong, were freed, and revolutionary papers were allowed to be printed and circulated inside Indo-China.

But the *détente* was short. The colonialists, whether left wing or right, found themselves the victims of a psychopathic disorder that once plagued only bulls but has since become endemic amongst humans. The most distressing aspect of rubiphobia[4] is that fascism promotes it almost as a religious concept; so that rubiphobists who may dislike all the other things fascism stands for are nevertheless driven into that camp. Thus the French colonialists, even those described as 'reliably anti-fascist', found themselves, in the final analysis, supporting the pro-fascist elements.

If, as Fall suggests, Ho did actually come to the Macao conference, he seems to have returned to Russia promptly; on this occasion not to engage in political work or training but to tackle once again the problem of his lungs, for which his hospitalization in Hong Kong, perhaps because of the hot humid climate, had been ineffective. In the summer of 1938 we therefore find him at Sochi, on the shores of the Black Sea. This was probably the nearest Ho had ever come to taking a holiday. From the date of certain articles in the ICP news-sheet in Saigon we find that he did, during this period, send in material, some of which contains contemporary references that indicate he read the daily newspapers. But for the most part, these months in the later part of 1938 seem to have been given over to convalescence.

He then made another trip to China, which he could now enter freely, not because of the Popular Front (which had already crumbled) but

[2] *Le Viet Minh*, p. 32.
[3] McLane, *op. cit.*, p. 216, indicates that the Comintern directed Ho to effect these changes at a party plenum in South China in July 1936.
[4] Hatred of red.

because the Japanese invasion of China in 1937 had forced Chiang into a partnership (albeit uneasy) with the Chinese communists. Ho was thus able to make open contact with the Communist forces. Nguyen Luong Bang tells us that 'as a member of an army unit, he pushed a cart from Sian to Yenan for five days on end'.[5]

This observation points up Ho's extensive travels. Had he never been a political leader and international communist, he might still deserve a certain fame as a traveller over vast distances in conditions varying from difficult to grim. In those days there was no air travel (at least, none available to Ho's particular needs). We have seen that via steamships he called at numerous ports along the African and Mediterranean shores, sailed to North and South America and visited England and France: all this was routine for someone able to bear the sort of hardships Asiatic seamen were expected to put up with. But in regard to general travel in the East, every mile was likely to require toil and sweat. Each visit to Moscow, for example, would have required that two-way Trans-Siberian trek: weeks of discomfort, heat or cold, bad food, vermin, dysentery – the inevitable penalties of over-crowding and chaos. To penetrate into Siam or China was likely to be even worse. In those days the traveller in either country soon came to the end of whatever railway happened to exist, and then had to proceed by pony, sampan or on foot, unless he could find an always-decrepit motor vehicle going that way. Merely to consider Ho's walk to Sian mentioned by Bang: the distance is about two hundred miles. If Bang is correct about the 'five days', that would be forty miles a day! We also have to take his word for it that Ho actually pushed a cart this vast distance; and this for a man not only just recovered from tuberculosis but aged forty-eight, when most of us have already put our feet up on the mantelpiece.[6]

Bang doesn't mention how Ho had reached Sian from Russia. This journey in itself would be an enterprise, whether one came eastwards through Turkestan and the Gobi Desert or, having made the Trans-Siberian journey, westwards from the China coast. Bang also doesn't mention what Ho was doing in the Eighth Route Army or why he went to Yenan. The fact that he was 'pushing a cart' indicates he was one of a guerrilla unit. It is probable he wanted to learn guerrilla tactics at first hand. But he may also have had a deeper purpose. After a few weeks in the Chinese Communist capital (then a collection of caves dug into the friable rock) he journeys south again in company with a group of guerrilla specialists. Their mission was, surprisingly, to help train Chiang's Kwangsi army in this same guerrilla warfare. We cannot but suspect that Ho himself organized this particular Trojan horse and that many of these specialists infiltrated even further south to train Giap and other Vietnamese guerrillas.

After getting into Kwangsi, Ho took a new pseudonym of Tran and proceeded westward to Kunming. This capital of Yunnan, China's south-west province bordering Burma and Vietnam, was later to

5 *Days with Ho Chi Minh*, p. 81.
6 When the author travelled overland from Hong Kong to Sian in 1941 the journey took two difficult weeks; and this would have been only one section of Ho's particular trip. Connecting railways had, of course, been cut.

become the Grand Central Station of the Far Eastern war. But at this earlier period it had no significance except as the terminus of a railway the French had built north-westwards from Hanoi. To prevent Jap penetration, the Chinese had cut the line at the border and blown the bridge across the river. But as the line operated on both sides of the gap it still offered a train ride for most of the journey; and any sort of train ride in the Far East is as good as a magic carpet. Many Vietnamese dissidents had thus assembled in Kunming. One of such dissidents was Vu Anh who had got a job in a local balsam products company.

I kept our comrades with my wages and secretly used the Company's shop as a liaison centre for the revolution. In January 1940, I was told by one of the Party Central Committee to look out for a Mr Tran. At the end of February, an elderly man dressed in European style entered the Company shop, made a routine inquiry in Chinese and then whispered to me in Vietnamese, 'My name is Tran. Let's go to the park and have a talk.'[7]

After this preliminary meeting it was arranged for 'Mr Tran' to see Pham Van Dong and Vo Nguyen Giap who lived a mile or two out of town. Dong, of course, had long been a trusted friend, but Ho had never previously met the man who, fifteen years later, was to out-manœuvre and defeat the French Army. Here is Giap's own version of the meeting:

One day, Phung Chi Kien[8] asked me to accompany him to Tsuy Hu where Vuong would be waiting for us. We walked leisurely along the Tsuy Hu bank and came across a thin middle-aged man wearing a European-style suit and a grey fur hat. Kien introduced him to me as 'Comrade Vuong'. I immediately recognized the man as Nguyen Ai Quoc. Compared with the photograph I had seen, he was much more lively, more alert-looking. I still remember that I had none of the sensations I expected from such a meeting. Instead, I found in him that simplicity of manner, that lucidity of character, which later, when I worked by his side, always had the same impact on me.[9]

It was arranged that Dong and Giap should now go to Yenan, to study both political and military technique. The difficulties of this trip, which Ho had accomplished as a matter of routine, are now made clear. The intending travellers first needed help from the Eighth Route Army. This meant going to their southern headquarters in Kweiyang, in itself a three-day journey by 'bus'. Then they had to wait for another 'bus' to Yenan. This term 'bus' needs explaining. In the China of that period it referred to any motorized vehicle which undertook a journey for pay-ing passengers, usually under state auspices. It might go twice a week, or once a month; it might go never. This depended on the availability of an internal combustion engine which, when installed inside a suitable

[7] *Days with Ho Chi Minh*, pp. 150/1.
[8] A well-known ICP leader later killed in an encounter with the Japs. See p. 69.
[9] *Days with Ho Chi Minh*, pp. 174/5.

contraption on wheels, could then be propelled along a road. Since no engines were manufactured in China, and since the Japs had sealed off most possibilities of importation they were in short supply. Adding to the difficulties, the roads over which these 'buses' had to travel were at best hard-packed dirt and at worst mere stony tracks. Even when the engine battled successfully, the tyres would succumb to a blow-out. This preamble explains Giap's next comments:

> As food supplies in a region situated deep in the country like Kweiyang were very difficult to find and the Party's finances were limited, we had to grow our own vegetables. Meat was very scarce. But the question of transportation was the greatest of our difficulties. *We had to wait a long time for a bus*.[10]

The distance from Kweiyang to Sian (from which Ho, we may recall, had walked his final 200 miles) is about 1,200 miles. It was hardly surprising that no bus was readily available to undertake this journey, which includes innumerable mountain passes, each with a score of suicidal hairpin bends. Small wonder that Dong and Giap never got that bus and hence never got to Yenan. This merely points up Ho's own travel accomplishments: we only once hear of his failing to go anywhere he wants.[11] As things turned out, Ho was just as well pleased to keep his two lieutenants on hand. Paris had fallen, the Germans had occupied France, and the consequent disruption of the Colonial administration in Indo-China would give the Vietnamese a special opportunity to further their cause.

Meanwhile, Ho had been helping Vu Anh with propaganda work, particularly with the writing and circulation of a newspaper. To promote it, Ho travelled up and down the railway line visiting the chain of bases. Never without a typewriter, he kept Vu Anh regularly supplied with articles. At one of the bases, Xi Xuyen, he called to see an agent named Hoang Quang Binh, whose hairdresser's shop served as a meeting place for the railway workers:

> It was late in the afternoon. I was doing a haircut when I saw two persons looking at me from across the street. I knew that one was actually Phung Chi Kien but did not know the other was Uncle Ho. I still remember that he wore a faded khaki suit and was clean shaven. Looking oldish and meek like an old countryman, but slender and sinewy, he easily went unnoticed had it not been for his very bright eyes.[12]

Ho and Phung Chi Kien stayed on to give talks to the railway workers and to start a training course for the Party cell members.

> The lectures given by Uncle were very concise. Explaining dialectical materialism, he quoted actual facts from the workers' situation. He

[10] *ibid.*, p. 177.   [11] See Chapter 7.
[12] *ibid.*, p. 136. It will be noted that almost everyone remarks on these bright eyes. Two other world figures who have evoked similar universal comment are Lenin and Picasso.

used simple words such as those of a story teller and always ended
his speech by asking whether and how well we understood him.
    Uncle would get up very early. Though the house was narrow and
the attic rickety, he still did physical training. Then he cleaned out
the room. A poor, dark and untidy attic thus became more orderly,
better aired and even seemed better lit.
    During the day, while I was busy cutting hair, he split firewood
and boiled rice, while Kien prepared vegetables. Even my wife, who
had grown perverse from a life of hard-bargaining, was very pleased
because Uncle helped her fetch and carry. He looked after my son
Hai even better than I did, putting him to bed, covering him several
times during the night, keeping him warm against pneumonia,
bathing and washing him many times and teaching him to be clean.[13]

Ho got them all to come along to the stream and bathe. Hoang also
notes that he was always fond of cleanliness:

> The first time I cut his hair, he told me 'You had better wash this
> apron often and you will get more customers. All work must be well
> done. The more so, since our shop only caters for workers.' [There
> was another hairdresser in the town who catered for 'clerks, train-
> masters and employees working in the French quarter'.] He was
> always very thrifty. He only smoked cigarettes he rolled himself,
> although ready-made cigarettes saved a lot of bother. Whenever I
> had money to spare I would buy some for him.
> At Xi Xuyen there was a very cruel station master who had a girl
> of about thirteen as a servant. He used to beat her most savagely.
> Infuriated, we wanted to give him a thrashing. Meanwhile, Uncle
> asked the girl about her native place and her parents, and we learned
> that she was an orphan sold by an uncle of hers to this train master.
> Nonplussed for a while, then sighing, Uncle said to us, 'Beating the
> cruel man would not remove the cause of the evil. That is why we
> have to wage a revolution.'[14]

On this occasion Ho stayed with Hoang about a month. It was to be
four years before they met again. Meanwhile, Ho (as we shall see) had
spent eighteen months in Chinese prisons. The strain of this is evident
in Hoang's continued story:

> One afternoon in late 1944, I was doing a haircut when I saw a thin,
> tired-looking old man stepping into my shop. Realizing to my
> surprise that he was Tran, I wanted to leave the customers who were
> waiting; but he told me to continue. He was dressed like a Chiang
> Kai-shek soldier with a cap covering his big forehead, a jacket
> patched with many pieces, and worn-out grass shoes bespattered
> with mud. He put down his blue bundle beside him. Seeing that
> Uncle was so tired, I inquired after his health. 'I am weary and even
> ill,' he said. 'But things are changing fast. I must toil along despite
> my illness.'

[13] *ibid.*, p. 138/9.
[14] *op. cit.*, p. 140.

Ho then told Hoang not about his life in prison (which he had already put behind him) but about the recent journey on his 800-mile trip from Kweilin, the point where he had been released. Famine was then raging, the countryside was full of hungry bandits. Although feverish with malaria, Ho had only a single threadbare blanket. This is one of the very few occasions when Ho reveals the hardships of his travels.

Hoang concludes his reminiscences with an account of his third meeting. It was August 1945 and the revolution had taken place. This time they met in the 'North Vietnam Palace'. Uncle inquired solicitously whether Hoang, who had just arrived in Hanoi, had everything he needed.

'Where are you staying? Have you had a meal? Are you all right for clothes?' He was as simple and friendly as in the past; not like the Head of State but the same old 'Uncle'. Though he lived in the splendid 'North Vietnam Palace' adorned with pictures, photos, standing mirrors and valuable old vases, he wore only a shirt, a pair of khaki trousers and white rubber sandals. Taking a packet of ready-made cigarettes from his pocket, he lit one for himself, put the rest in my breast pocket and buttoned it up. He still remembered that I was the hairdresser who now and then had bought some of these cigarettes for him.[15]

[15] *ibid.*, p. 148.

7 Nationalist

In front of the gate, the guard stands with his rifle.
Above, untidy clouds are carrying away the moon.
The bed-bugs are swarming round like army-tanks on manœuvres,
While the mosquitoes form squadrons, attacking like fighter-planes.
My heart travels a thousand li towards my native land.
My dream intertwines with sadness like a skein of a thousand threads.
Innocent, I have now endured a whole year in prison.
Using my tears for ink, I turn my thoughts into verses.

In 1939 World War II began with the Nazi invasion of Poland, whose
territory the UK and France were committed to defend. For two years
this war, later to become global, was limited to Europe. But already in
1931 the Japanese had on their account invaded Manchuria (part of
China) and in 1937 they had attacked Shanghai and penetrated into
central China. This invasion was resisted both by the Chinese Nationalists (Kuomintang) under Chiang Kai-shek and the Chinese Red Army
under Mao Tse-tung; in neither case very successfully, since the
Japanese had superiority in every form of *matériel.*

The Far Eastern map at this time showed India (including Pakistan),
Ceylon, Burma, Malaya, Singapore, Hong Kong, North Borneo and
Southern New Guinea as British possessions, with the French occupying Indo-China, and the Dutch the East Indies (Indonesia). Although
the Americans had long conceded Philippine Independence they vir-
tually controlled its economy. Various nations had concessions in
Chinese treaty-ports. The Japanese, victorious over the Chinese in 1894
(when they wrested Formosa, now Taiwan), victorious over the Russians
in 1905 (which enabled them in a five-year period to wrest Korea), and
now again victorious over China (from whom they had snatched
Manchuria), had ambitions to control all Asia in place of the Western
powers then in possession.

In 1940 Hitler overran France, and the Japanese saw an immediate
opportunity to penetrate Indo-China, which could no longer look for
any assistance from Metropolitan France. They began by demanding
only the control of the Tonkin border with China, as a means of
implementing their war against Chiang Kai-shek. The French colonial
administration, at first under General Catroux, then under Admiral
Jean Decoux, found themselves with only two alternatives: to resist
overwhelming Japanese odds or to submit. After making the second
choice they soon found what was clearly inevitable: the Japanese
imposed one demand after another until they controlled almost everything concerned with Defence and Foreign Affairs and could exercise
a veto over whatever the French were allowed to retain.

The Vietnamese national movement thus found itself facing two
opponents, of which the Japanese were likely to be worse, since as
exploiters they were not only equally ruthless but better organized.
From the communist-international point of view things were made even

more difficult for Ho: because of the ramifications of the Hitler-Stalin pact Japan was not yet considered an 'imperialist enemy'. Since Germany and Japan had an *entente*, Russia and Japan necessarily had a policy of at least cautious toleration. The Comintern therefore promoted neutrality towards the Japs. Ho found he had to steer a careful course while at the same time stepping up his revolutionary plans in anticipation of a new twist when the Allies staged the inevitable counter-attack.

It was probably because of this impasse that from this time on Ho became less obviously an agent of the Comintern and more a nationalist striving for his country's independence. As we have tried to show, international communism had been for Ho a means, not an end, although the two were inseparable, since he believed that only within the framework of Marxism-Leninism could nationalist freedom be achieved. He utilized the Comintern in the way that, for instance, a traveller might be said to utilize his nationality: although finding it convenient to vaunt his passport while travelling, when finally in Rome he may find it better to do as the Romans do.

Ho had now spent twenty years in learning the techniques of revolution and in organizing his compatriots. He had sought out and indoctrinated these compatriots in places as wide apart as Shanghai, Canton, Hong Kong and Siam. But now most of these trained revolutionaries were either inside Vietnam or assembled in that part of China bordering Vietnam – the provinces of Yunnan and Kwangsi. Of these two areas Kwangsi offered the more accessible routes and would clearly make the better spearhead from which to launch the revolution. It was therefore important to establish an *entente* with the Chinese hierarchy in that province. Both Chang Fa-kwei, the Kwangsi warlord, and Li Chi-sen, leader of Chiang Kai-shek's army in the area, had liberal leanings. Furthermore they both recognized that the Japanese military presence in Indo-China constituted a threat that required full co-operation with all anti-Japanese groups. On a purely realistic basis, therefore, they saw in Ho a useful ally.

Early in 1941 Ho took advantage of this possible co-operation by setting up a base at Ching-hsi, a Chinese border town offering a convenient route into Vietnam. That Ho had no illusions about the dependability and permanence of this liaison is shown by his instructions to Giap:

> We must have a clear-cut understanding regarding this question. Only the Soviet Red Army and the Chinese Red Army are fraternal to us and are really our allies. We shall welcome them. The Chiang Kai-shek troops are anti-Japanese to some extent, but their nature is reactionary. In the present Nationalist-Communist collaboration they talk of fighting the Japanese, but actually seek all possible means to destroy the Communists. We must always bear in mind their reactionary character; any other attitude would be dangerous.[1]

From Ching-hsi, Ho and his associates were able without much difficulty to slip across the border. Vu Anh fills in some quizzical

[1] *Days with Ho Chi Minh*, pp. 178/9.

details regarding this trip. Part of the journey was by sampan, which – as usual with any form of transport in China – was so overcrowded that it offered cover to possible spies. Ho therefore pretended to be a Chinese Press correspondent speaking French:

> Dong was his interpreter, and everybody took him for a journalist. The boat was going upstream and had to be pulled. Uncle took part in pulling the boat.[2] He only answered questions when translated to him. A certain Vietnamese woman, being thirsty, was about to drink river water. Ho told her, in French, with Dong interpreting, 'Don't drink that or you'll get stomach-ache, chew on sugar-cane instead.' But when one of our comrades had his coat burnt by a cigarette, Uncle forgot his cover and called in Vietnamese, 'Mind the fire!' Later, we used to have a good laugh over this story.[3]

This would appear to have been Ho's first entry into Vietnam since he sailed out of Saigon thirty years earlier.[4]

All this area on both sides of the border is picturesque karst[5] country, with sugar-loaf hills made famous by generations of Chinese painters, and tributary rivers gouging caves out of the limestone. It was in one such cave, thickly forested with stalactites, that Vu Anh had discovered a suitable hideout[6] for the revolutionary headquarters. Two circles of guards protected the cave, and Ho had a 'personal guard'.

> Recommending secrecy in all our work he would emphasize, 'Secrecy means to hear nothing, to see nothing, to know nothing. If a stranger asks you anything, your only answer must be: I hear nothing, I see nothing, I know nothing.' Then he added, 'But no secrecy is possible with the masses, who give us protection and intelligence.'[7]

Giap also describes their life at this time:

> From our cave we could see here and there sheets of limpid water, and a stream meandering round the mountain base. Uncle called it the Lenin stream. Every day he woke early and stirred up all of us. After physical exercise, he usually took a bath before starting work,

[2] Ho seems to have made a point of taking, whenever possible, a physical role: he pulls sampans, pushes carts, chops wood, fetches food, washes children, cleans rooms, performs exercises, cooks meals and cultivates gardens. By challenging his physique in this fashion he no doubt accumulated 'a sackful of diamonds' against the severe hardship of his later life.

[3] *op. cit.*, p. 157.

[4] Some writers have disputed this. Robert Shaplen, for instance, states that in the twenties he made brief trips to Hanoi and on one occasion narrowly escaped from the French *Sûreté* by 'stripping to the waist, grabbing a rickshaw and pulling an old lady with vegetables in her lap beyond the security cordon'. *The Lost Revolution*, p. 38.

[5] So called from the district of Karst in Jugoslavia, characterized by almost unique formations resulting from erosion of prevailing limestone.

[6] At Bac Bo, just inside Vietnam.

[7] *Days with Ho Chi Minh*, p. 159.

despite the cold weather. He always kept himself busy – he either worked, held meetings, studied, gathered firewood or visited the nearby villages. Sometimes he organized a political training course for the old people or taught the children to read and write. If he did not go out he worked all day long at his 'desk', a flat rock near the stream, and would stop only for meals. At night we slept on beds made of branches which of course were neither soft nor warm. It was very cold at night. Sometimes we had to make a fire and sit around it until daybreak. During these hours, Uncle would tell us the history of the world's people who had lived through many wars and revolutions. He foretold that within four or five years, the war in our country would enter its decisive phase and that would be a very favourable time for our revolution. This he told us again and again, like folk tales, while we sat around our fire in the cave at night.[8]

And it was in this same cave that in May 1941 the famous Vietminh League (VML) was born. The full name was Viet Nam Doc Lap Dong Minh (League for Vietnamese Independence); but Ho decided that the shorter name would be easier for the peasants who would form the bulk of the membership. The Vietminh was set up by a nucleus of ICP members. In expounding its programme on 6 June Ho addressed an appeal to 'Patriots of all ages and all types, intellectuals, peasants, workers, businessmen, soldiers', in which he summarized the existing political situation: France having been defeated by the Germans, the French colonials had surrendered to the Japanese and were giving them full support in continuing the policy of Vietnamese exploitation.[9] The hour had now almost struck for raising the standard of insurrection. National salvation, said Ho, must be the common goal. Every Vietnamese should make his contribution. Those with money should give it. Strong men should give their muscular strength, talented men should contribute their skills. Ho appealed for unity and readiness but made no proposals for immediate action.

He ended his appeal on a single Marxist note: '*The world revolution will conquer.*' This appeal came in 1941 just before Hitler's attack on Russia and it curiously anticipates that fatal invasion, which, from the communist point of view, transformed an 'imperialist' war into a 'people's' war; so that from then on any action against the Japs and their Vichy-French allies became, in communist eyes, part of the '*world revolution*'. But in general we might say that with the inauguration of the Vietminh Ho took his first step towards detaching himself from Soviet domination. While continuing a declared adherence to international communism we find that he really beats his own path as he sees fit; and when he has occasion to seek Soviet help he applies not as a Comintern agent but as an independent adjuvant.

[8] *ibid.*, pp. 186/7.
[9] 'After the Japs came in, 60,000 French colonials went on living much as before. Little of the old grand manner had to be foregone. Even business went on much as usual. . . . In all Asia, French Indo-China was the one efficient Japanese political success. The French did their work for them.' William Lederer, *The Anguished American*, Gollancz 1969, p. 69.

Ho next wrote up a series of pamphlets on guerrilla tactics which were distributed to the forward units fanning out from Caobang further south. A forward base was also set up in the jungle near Lam Son. Ho and Giap lived in a house on poles built on a mountain slope. This was an improvement over Bac Bo.[10] The house was an improvement but the diet was much as before: maize and wild bananas. It was while they were staying here that they were told that Phung Chi Kiem had been killed by a Jap patrol sent to hunt them down. 'This heart-rending news came to us,' writes Giap, 'when we were on our way to a conference. Uncle stopped suddenly and tears streamed down his cheeks. Only after a while could he go on.'

Throughout Giap's account of this period we are made aware that comradeship and a sense of purpose more than repaid them for all their perils and hardships.

Every time we returned to our headquarters we felt as if we had returned to our own home, a home where revolutionaries lived together like brothers, knowing that they must endure hardships and remembering their task would be long. The movement was nevertheless developing strongly. Each monthly military-training course drew in a fresh batch of fifty or sixty. Deep in the forest there was soon everything: lecture hall, dining-room, dormitory and a training ground large enough for hundreds of persons. About this time Uncle went abroad. Time passed rapidly as we threw all our energies into our work. Then one day, when we had fought our way as far as the Mgan Son district and were organizing a training course for local cadres, we received an urgent letter from Pham Van Dong asking us to return immediately to Cao Bang. Upon arrival we learned that Uncle had been arrested in China by Chiang Kai-shek troops and had died in prison.

Months went by without their being able to get further news. It was the depths of winter and up in the mountains the nights were bitterly cold. This added to their general despair: no more Uncle to cheer them up with folk tales round the fire! Then suddenly – a letter from China. They at once recognized Ho's writing. It was a very simple message: 'I wish all brothers at home good health. Hope you are striving in your work. I am quite well.' And there followed a poem:

The clouds embrace the peaks, the peaks embrace the clouds,
The river below shines like a mirror, spotless and clean.
On the crest of the Western Mountains, my heart stirs as I wander
Looking towards the Southern sky and dreaming of old friends.

Between astonishment and joy Giap called for the man who had brought the earlier message. It appeared that he had heard about Ho's death from the prison guard. He had asked whether Ho was really in this prison, and the man had said 'dead', he had said it several times, impatiently. Then Giap worked it out that the man had really said 'yes' and kept saying yes. The word for dead sounds like 'sirla' and the word

[10] *ibid.*, p. 191.

for yes like 'shirla'. 'As a result we had been tormented for months by pain and sorrow.'[11]

What seems to have happened was that Ho entered China intending to go up to Chungking and contact Chiang Kai-shek. His object is not made clear, but he perhaps felt that the Vietminh League could now offer Chiang effective help against the Japs. But in the meantime Chang Fa-kwei had revived the VNDDQ (the pro-Kuomintang Vietnamese group); and either wanted to suppress the Vietminh or bring it strictly under his control. Thus Ho had become a wanted man. He seems to have sensed the need for caution in passing through Chang Fa-kwei's domain, and before setting out to cross the border took a new pseudonym – the one that was now to last him to the end of his days. Vu Anh tells us that he had visiting cards made up with 'Ho Chi Minh'[12] in the middle, 'press correspondent' in one corner and 'Vietnam-overseas Chinese' in another.[13]

To infiltrate the Japanese lines inside Vietnam Ho adopted a different disguise:

> He walked 50 kilometres from Lam Son to Bac Bo in daytime. Le Quang Ba, his liaison agent, preceded him. Clad in 'tribesmen' clothes, a walking stick in his hand, Uncle went behind, affecting to be a blind man. Having passed the frontier, he took a Chinese friend as a liaison agent but the latter had no papers and was arrested. Uncle met a similar fate. Both were put in the same prison, where the Chinese liaison agent died afterwards.[14]

This laconic account is all we have concerning the actual arrest. Nor have we much to go on concerning the charges against him and his subsequent fourteen months in prison. If Chang Fa-kwei arrested him merely to impose full control it seems curious that Ho never mentions this: there is nothing in *Prison Diary* (see below) to indicate that he was interrogated or subjected to the kind of organized duress that might exact 'co-operation'. Having entered China under an assumed name and without proper papers, at a time when the Nationalists were

---

11 *ibid.*, pp. 195/6. Perhaps because of translation and re-translation, Lacouture (*op. cit.*, p. 61) gives what seems an inaccurate version.

12 'Ho' is a fairly common Chinese name which the Vietnamese leader had already used when going to Yenan. 'Chi' means approximately 'coming from the heart'. 'Minh' is the Chinese character for 'very bright', being composed of pictographs of the sun and moon. 'Chi Minh' together thus has the meaning of 'bringing brightness' or perhaps 'bringing enlightenment'.

13 This may seem curious but was at the time fairly standard practice when travelling in China. Almost every traveller carried visiting cards. Merely to *say* one's name when there were for instance so many different 'Chans' or 'Wongs' would have been inadequate; and the variations of dialect added to the confusion. The written character on the other hand could only mean that particular 'Chan' or 'Wong' and would be understood regardless of dialect. In addition, all Chinese people liked to know who and what you were so this was usually put on the visiting cards.

14 *Days with Ho Chi Minh*, p. 165.

perilously at war with Japan as well as engaged in clandestine suppression of communists, Ho left himself open to the charge of spying. His subsequent treatment, although grievous, does not appear to have been worse than that inflicted on other prisoners. He was marched from gaol to gaol, often in chains, half frozen, and half starved. It seems likely that only his earlier ascetic discipline could have carried him through fourteen months of this.

From time to time he managed to send out messages such as the one mentioned, or more often written in rice water on the margins of newspapers (developed with tincture of iodine such writing shows up brown).[15] He also wrote the poems that have later come to be called *Prison Diary*.[16] These poems, some 120 in all, are not really a diary, but impressions; some descriptive, others more abstract. Ho wrote them, not in Vietnamese, but in classical Chinese. Perhaps he felt it was better that his guards should be able to read what he was writing; perhaps he merely felt the need to exercise the discipline, both intellectual and artistic, that the writing of poems in classical Chinese requires.

The circumstances of Ho's release from imprisonment are no clearer than those of his capture. Ho himself offers no lucid explanation and his commentators (such as Vu Anh) are equally vague. The probable reason for this vagueness is that neither Ho nor his associates could easily explain that he had probably bought himself out of prison by agreeing to co-operate with his captors. In any event we find him immediately upon his release joining the Vietnam Revolutionary League (usually called the Dong Minh Hoi) which had been set up by Chang Fa-kwei.

We have seen (page 66) that Chang, acting for Chiang Kai-shek, was anxious even as early as 1941 to get co-operation of anti-Japanese groups, including Ho. In 1943, at the Cairo Summit Conference, Roosevelt had shown himself to be against the re-occupation of Indo-China by the French and had secretly agreed that Chiang might consider Tonkin to be included in his own sphere of influence. It had therefore been essential that China should get a prior foothold to offset the possibility of facing a hostile population. When Chang Fa-kwei found that not only was the VNQDD ineffective but that he could not get the Vietminh under his control he had set up this new group, the Dong Minh Hoi, under a Vietnamese nationalist named Nguyen Hai Than, whose only qualification for the post was his pro-Chinese record. Chang had hoped that without Ho's presence the Vietminh would crumble, while the Dong Minh Hoi would flourish. Both these hopes proved abortive, and Chang found himself not only with an ineffective group under a leader having neither ability nor influence but facing a powerful group, the Vietminh, able to sway a large section of the Vietnamese population and now pitted against him because he had imprisoned its leader. The compromise apparently arrived at was that

---

15 *ibid.*, p. 165.
16 *Prison Diary*, Foreign Languages Publishing House, Hanoi, 1965. (Translated by Aileen Palmer.) In addition to those quoted at the chapter headings, a selection will be found in Appendix B.

Ho should be released and the Vietminh and the Dong Minh Hoi united under his own leadership. On the face of it, Ho had come out on top, and this despite fourteen months' debilitation in gaol.

But the new arrangements detonated several small explosions. In the first place, there were, in the Dong Minh Hoi, elements vehemently anti-communist as well as others essentially pro-Japanese. Secondly, there was in Indo-China a pro-Vichy French 'government' under Admiral Decoux, furiously anti-nationalist. Thirdly there was in China the Free-French Military Mission (FMM) sent by de Gaulle, which if not furiously anti-nationalist, was certainly anti-Vietminh.

To try and calm this rising storm, Chang Fa-kwei in March of 1944, having privily discussed with Ho the expediency of new arrangements, called a conference in Liuchow of all the Vietnamese nationalists. Ho was by no means ready for a showdown: his immediate need was to keep the Viet Minh operating. If his resignation as leader of the Dong Minh Hoi would pacify the hostile elements he was happy to concede it. Another, safer, Vietnamese nationalist was therefore substituted as top man. Ho in any case had a more urgent task, this time concerned with the Americans.

In December 1941 the Japanese had launched their surprise attack on the United States naval base in Pearl Harbor as well as on key British bases in Singapore and Hong Kong. They had thus hoped to render the US and UK striking forces so ineffective that an overwhelming Japanese conquest of the Far East would leave Japan invulnerable. That they came close to accomplishing this object is testimony to the skill of their blitzkrieg. The British, already sore-pressed in Europe, had been almost powerless to strike back at the Japanese attack, and even the United States was for two whole years largely confined to recouping losses in the Pacific.

It was thus not until late 1943 that the Americans could spare any considerable resources for operations on the Asiatic mainland. The three most important units were: the air force under General Claire Chennault (easily the most significant); the Services of Supply, largely aiding the Chinese forces; and the Office of Strategic Services (OSS),[17] a clandestine group operating intelligence, counter-intelligence, under-cover propaganda, and sabotage.

By mid-1944 this third group had already sent out teams against the Japanese, having enlisted Chinese agents (from all political camps) who in some instances were trained and supplied for independent ventures. As the US fleet battered its costly advance from the Pacific Ocean into the South China Sea, Indo-China with its 1,500-mile coastline took on a new significance: OSS therefore began to investigate similar operations in this area; and Ho saw in this the opportunity to get support for his own guerrilla teams operating against the Japanese.

Meanwhile, however, Giap and others down at forward base had been agitating for extended action. Ho hurried down to curb their impatience. The time for general insurrection, he impressed upon them, was not yet ripe.[18] Instead of promoting an uprising Ho launched, in

[17] From this group there later (postwar) emerged the Central Intelligence Agency (CIA).
[18] McLane, *op. cit.*, p. 263.

December 1944, the Vietnam Propaganda and Liberation Unit, whose object was to arouse the population and enlist its support against that time when the bugle call sounded. Full-scale military action, Ho emphasized to Giap, could only be effective against superior forces if *the local population were on your side*. Parallel with this, of course, the Vietminh units could continue to enlarge their own guerrilla operations. 'Be secret, rapid, active,' Ho enjoined, 'now here, now there, arriving unexpectedly and leaving unnoticed.'[19] Having tied up all loose ends, Ho said *au revoir* and started off on the long and arduous trek to Kunming, by then the American main base. It so happened that while he was on his way through Caobang, one of his guerrilla units rescued an American pilot, Lieutenant Shaw, who had parachuted into the jungle when his plane had been shot down by the Japs. 'The French and Japanese actively searched for him, but the revolutionary masses protected him and brought him to Pham Van Dong's office in the region of Nuoc Hai where he was sent to meet Uncle.'[20]

Ho instructed a team to take Shaw over the border and deliver him safely into American hands. He could hardly have guessed that this action would prove a magic key to open doors otherwise impregnable.

[19] *Days with Ho Chi Minh*, p. 203.
[20] *ibid.*, p. 167.

8 Gambler

Everything evolves, it is the cycle of nature:
After the rainy days, the fine weather comes.
In an instant, the whole world shakes off its damp clothes,
Thousands of li of mountains unfurl their brocade carpet.
Under the warm sun and the clean wind, the flowers smile,
In the big trees with branches washed clean, the birds make chorus.
Warmth fills the heart of man and life reawakens.
Bitterness now makes way for happiness.
This is how nature wills it.

As with the run of luck in any gambling game, there are times when fate
conspires against you and other times, more rare, when she throws you
all four aces. Up to this point Ho had seldom had good luck as against
the solid accomplishments resulting from his own toil. There had been
that lucky time when he was helped to escape from the Hong Kong
hospital; there had also been his luck in not actually dying in the
Chinese gaol. One might say, however, that both these manifestations
of good fortune were negative rather than positive: they gave him a
chance to go on living without adding anything to his progress. But
around this period, that is, early 1945, the stars were all in his favour.[1]
With the rescue of Lt. Shaw, Ho had received his first ace. He was
to wait two months for his second. Reaching Kunming sometime in
February he at once endeavoured to contact the Americans. He particularly wanted to meet General Chennault. There were several reasons
for this, the most significant being the prestige of the US Fourteenth
Air Force: apart from Chinese Communist forces in the north and
Chinese Nationalist forces elsewhere (both fighting the enemy with
inadequate, obsolete equipment), it was strictly the US air force that
represented the Allied striking forces in China. There were no French
or British planes, and no ground forces of any Allied nation except the
Chinese. The Vietnamese patriots therefore saw in Chennault a great
leader actively on their side. His reputation, furthermore, had been
almost mythically enhanced as former chief of the famous 'Flying
Tigers', that body of US volunteer aviators who, with a minimum of
planes, had a year or two earlier halted Japanese bombing attacks on
Chinese cities. At that time Ho was still able to think of American
leaders as potentially anti-colonial, open-minded and approachable.
Not having been to Moscow for two whole years and no doubt being
out of touch with power politics he could scarcely know that following
the death of Roosevelt the American government under Truman had

[1] Regarding this good fortune, Lacouture remarks (*Ho Chi Minh*, p. 78), 'Ho
and his colleagues must have been devoid of the smallest religious sense, or
they would surely have been terrified by the almost miraculous nature of
their rise to power.' This seems a strange comment to make about men who
were confirmed Marxists and sceptics.

decided to re-establish French domination in Indo-China, thus by-
passing Vietnamese Independence.[2]

When Ho applied to see Chennault he was politely shown the door.
Nobody would credit his story about having engineered the escape of
Shaw, who had by this time gone back home. Ho's attempts to contact
OSS were almost as futile. This organization was not quite ready to
operate inside Vietnam with its own teams; and following the new
Truman directive, it did not wish at this stage to quarrel with the
French by backing 'natives'.

Ho's second ace came from a quite different direction. For some time
now the Japs had been getting more and more disgruntled with the
French inside Vietnam: some of these, they discovered, were helping
the Allied intelligence networks; others were offering their services to
de Gaulle's Military Mission. But the final insult to Japan came when
large numbers of pro-Vichy Frenchmen, whom the Japanese considered
loyal to their cause, started plotting a resistance movement. The French
Colonial Administration had by now realized that they had backed the
wrong horse: the Allies were going to win the war; and the Vichy-
French record inside Vietnam was going to look very black indeed. A
last minute effort had to be made to establish an anti-Japanese stand
that would give Decoux's administration a face-saving front.[3] Unfortunately for these embryonic patriots the Japanese got wind of their
plan. On 9 March they arrested in one swoop every Frenchman of
importance and thus effectively destroyed all that was left of French
power. This coup meant that one of Ho's two enemies was now effectively
hors de combat. Giap immediately declared Japan the sole enemy.
Vietminh units were even directed to help any Frenchmen wanting to
oppose 'the common enemy'. The Vietnamese were thus able to present
themselves as part of the common Allied front.

Upon learning of this crisis Ho was anxious to get back to Vietnam,
but not yet resigned to his failure in making a link with the Americans.
Indeed, he felt that to return to his base without having effected this
would now more than ever be a set-back, since the French, having been
forced into an irrevocable anti-Japanese position, would themselves
become entitled to American aid. It was at this point that Ho got his
third ace. And since I myself delivered it, I shall need to explain the
background of this circumstance.

I had been working for OSS in China for a year when in 1944 I was
directed by them to work with an independent group operating a network inside Indo-China with Free-French civilian agents. This group
was known as GBT, from the initials of the three Allied civilians who
ran it: L. L. Gordon, a Canadian, Harry Bernard, an American, and
Frank Tan, a Chinese-American. Formerly employed by an oil
company in Saigon, these three men, all admirable in their different
ways, had utilized their French contacts so well that no other intelligence group, either military or civilian, had equalled their record of
information collected and disseminated. Their reports were distributed
to all Allied intelligence centres. In the beginning the British (from
India) supplied the funds and equipment, the Chinese supplied personnel

---

[2] This was confirmed and amplified at the Potsdam Conference (see p. 86).
[3] See for example *From Colonialism to Communism*, pp. 61/2.

(such as cipher clerks, radio operators at base, and office staff), and the
US Fourteenth Air Force gave various small services. Some time later
GBT received money and equipment from OSS as well as from
another US organization, Air Ground Aid Services (AGAS), whose
work was divided between the rescue of downed pilots, liaison with
Prisoners of War, and collection of intelligence.

When OSS decided to extend their operations into Indo-China they
wanted to take over GBT, and as a first step assigned me to work with
the group. GBT were against losing their independence, especially to
OSS, whose methods Gordon considered autocratic. In February 1945
he went to Washington in hopes of preserving the independence of his
group, leaving Bernard and myself to run GBT, with Tan as third man.
But while Gordon was gone the fast-increasing pace of events forced a
decision; and as a compromise the GBT group was transferred to
AGAS along with my own services.

Scarcely had this been arranged when the Japanese coup of 9 March
silenced the GBT and all existing networks. This meant no information
coming in about targets, air defences and Japanese troop movements,
and no weather reports. GHQ therefore directed me to replace our lost
French agents with a Vietnamese network.

Kunming was full of Vietnamese (then called Annamites) but as we
had previously been warned not to use them we had no idea which ones
might be considered both useful and trustworthy. AGAS told me of an
old Annamite who was reported not only to have helped a downed
pilot escape but also to be connected with a large political group. It was
said that he was still in Kunming and occasionally could be found at
the American Office of War Information, where he read everything
from *Time* magazine to the *Encyclopaedia Americana*. I left word with
one of my friends to try and arrange a meeting, and a day or so later I
got a message that this old Annamite, whose name was Ho, would
meet me there that afternoon. My diary for 17 March 1945 reads:

Ho came along with a younger man named Fam. Ho wasn't what I
expected. In the first place he isn't really 'old': his silvery wisp of
beard suggests age, but his face is vigorous and his eyes bright and
gleaming. We spoke in French. It seems he has already met Hall,
Glass and de Sibour,[4] but got nowhere with any of them. I asked him
what he had wanted of them. He said – only recognition of his group
(called Vietminh League or League for Independence). I had vaguely
heard of this as being communist, and asked him about it. Ho said
that the French call all Annamites communists who want independence. I told him about our work and asked whether he'd like to
help us. He said they might be able to but had no radio operators
nor of course any equipment. We discussed taking in a radio and
generator and an operator. Ho said a generator would make too much
noise – the Japs were always around. Couldn't we use the type of set
with battery, such as the Chinese use? I explained they were too weak
for distant operation, especially when the batteries run down. I asked
him what he'd want in return for helping us. Arms and medicines, he
said. I told him the arms would be difficult, because of the French.

[4] OSS officers.

We discussed the problem of the French. Ho insisted that the Independence League are only anti-Jap. I was impressed by his clear-cut talk; Buddha-like composure except movements with wrinkled brown fingers. Fam made notes. It was agreed we should have a further meeting. They wrote their names down in Chinese characters which were romanized into Fam Fuc Pao and Ho Tchih Ming.[5]

After this meeting Bernard and Tan agreed that if something could be worked out we might send Ho back into Vietnam accompanied by one of our Chinese radio operators. It was also suggested that Tan might go along with him too. Three days later I was ready to arrange this:

20 March

Had a second meeting with the Annamites in the Indo-China cafe on Chin Pi Street. It seems that the proprietor is a friend of theirs. We sat upstairs and drank coffee filtered in the French style, strong and quite good. The room was empty but Ho said customers might come in. We agree to use certain terms: Chinese to be called 'friends', Americans 'brothers', French 'neutrals', Japs 'occupants', Annamites 'natives'. Ho said that in regard to taking down two Chinese, one of them American-Chinese, this might be difficult because the latter, certainly, would be easy to identify. Ho's group are inclined to be suspicious of the Chinese. Since there are no Annamite radio operators, the Chinese operator is of course inevitable. But instead of taking Tan, he'd rather go with this one man and then later we could drop in an American officer. Would I go myself? I said I would. Ho said his group would give me every welcome. We then discussed supplies. Fam mentioned the 'high explosives' that Hall had told him about. I tried to soft pedal this, but agreed we might later drop in light weapons, medicines and further radio sets. Our own operator could train some of Ho's men to use these. Ho also wants to meet Chennault. I agreed to arrange this if he would agree not to ask him for anything: neither supplies nor promises about support. Ho agreed. The old man wears Chinese-type cotton trousers and buttoned-to-the-neck jacket, sand-coloured, not blue. His sandals are the strap type they usually wear in Indo-China. His little beard is silvery, but his eyebrows are light-brown going grey at the top edge and his hair is still almost black but receding. The young man, Fam, wears a western-style suit and has enormous cheek-bones and a powerful chin. They both talk quietly but sometimes burst into chuckles. We seem to get on well together.

Meanwhile, our investigations into Ho's Vietminh group revealed that the French did indeed classify them as communist, although

[5] When I entered Ho on our list of agents I gave him the code name of 'Lucius', but amongst ourselves we used to call him 'Old Man Ho' not because he was really old (55 at the time) but to help us distinguish him from another Ho we had working for us. The one or two photographs taken of him at this time make him look younger because poor focusing takes out the lines from his face and the wisp of grey beard scarcely registers.

the Chinese merely called them 'tricky'. We asked AGAS to check
with GHQ-Chungking to get clearance. The instructions came back to
'get a net regardless'; we were not to be concerned about French-
native politics. After arranging for Ho to be presented to Chennault
as the 'native' who had helped rescue Shaw,[6] I took Tan along to
meet Ho at the place where he and Fam had a room above a candle
shop,

> the downstairs bristling with tapers, red, white and orange, with a
> tub of wax simmering on a stove at the back. Ho and Tan hit it off
> well, so the old man agreed to take him along. Tan is now getting
> ready for his trip. Bernard urges him to take only what's necessary:
> a radio, a pistol, a few small gifts. But Tan insists he must have a load
> of stuff: supplies give you face, he says. So he's started collecting an
> armory.

The meeting with Chennault came a few days later:

> Bernard and I were due to collect Ho at ten-thirty 29 March for the
> appointment at eleven. I noticed that Ho had replaced the missing
> button on his cotton jacket, no doubt to celebrate the occasion.
> Presenting ourselves at Chennault's outer office we are told that the
> general is engaged. Meanwhile a secretary appears and assures us
> the general won't be long. She is wearing a smart GI-drill-type jacket
> and skirt. Five minutes later we are shown into Chennault's office,
> where Doreen brings forward two chairs while Chennault himself
> places a third, very *kerchee*.[7] Then he goes to sit behind his desk the
> size of a double bed. A curious quintet: Chennault in a smart uniform
> complete with medals; Bernard in khaki shorts and shirt; me in a
> gabardine bush jacket and Marine Corps cap; old man Ho in cotton
> tunic and sandals; Doreen in her khaki get-up probably made by
> Saks Fifth Avenue and flown out by special plane. Chennault told
> Ho how grateful he was about the saved pilot. Ho said he would
> always be glad to help the Americans and particularly to help General
> Chennault for whom he had the greatest admiration. They exchanged
> talk about the *Flying Tigers*. Chennault was pleased the old man knew
> about this. We talked about saving more pilots. Nothing was said
> about the French, or about politics. I heaved a sigh of relief as we
> started to leave. Then Ho said he had a small favour to ask the
> general. 'Here we go boys, hold your hats', was written all over
> Bernard's face. But all Ho wanted was the general's photograph.
> There's nothing Chennault likes more than giving his photograph.
> So he presses the bell and in comes Doreen again. In due course it's
> some other girl who produces a folder of eight-by-ten glossies. 'Take
> your pick,' says Chennault. Ho takes one and asks would the general

---

[6] Robert Shaplen writes (*The Lost Revolution*, p. 33) that when Ho had tried
to contact Chennault, the general 'was warned by his KMT friends to steer
clear of him'. On one occasion he 'unwittingly had Ho introduced to him
as an old Vietnamese guide. Nothing came of that'. As we shall see, something very definitely did.

[7] The Chinese word for 'formally polite'.

be so kind as to sign it? Doreen produces a Parker 51 and Chennault writes across the bottom, 'Yours Sincerely, Claire L. Chennault'. And out we all troop into Kunming's sparkling air.[8]

As we shall see, it was by waving this photograph like a magic wand that Ho was later to produce a magnificent rabbit. But Chennault never heard about it.

Bernard arranged with 14th Air Force 'Ops' for two L-5's, the small taxi-planes we were then using. Ho was to fly down to the border in one plane with Mac Sin, the Chinese radio operator. A day or two later Tan was to fly in the other with all the equipment. There was an air strip at Ching-hsi, and they would have to walk in from there. Fam was to stay in Kunming for liaison. When I went to see Ho about these arrangements he asked for one further favour: six new Colt .45 automatic pistols in their original wrappings.[9]

When Bernard and I took Ho to the airfield and put him aboard the little crate that had to fly him across 300 miles of mountains and jungle he mentioned that this was only the third time he had flown. About a week later, Mac Sin having established radio contact with us, we learned the following: Ho himself had already crossed the border and had reached his cave base. He had sent back twenty of his men to escort Tan and Mac Sin inside and give them protection, not only against the Japs but against bandits. Some time later we received the first courier report from Tan:

The escorts arrived on 15 April and the next morning at 04.00 hours we set out dressed as border smugglers with all equipment carried in bamboo baskets so as to arouse normal suspicion of being illicit border traders. We walked parallel to the border until 15.00 hours, had our meal, waited until dark and then turned towards the border. This stretch of the journey was notorious for banditry so we unpacked and carried our arms while crossing the border.

He went on to describe the difficult and dangerous journey that finally brought them to Ho's base in the cave at Bac Bo: a mere hut in the entrance by a waterfall. To this hut members of the Vietminh League would come for consultations. 'As near as I can judge,' wrote Tan, 'this League is quite powerful and has several hundred followers.

---

[8] Chennault, essentially the Southern gentleman, invariably treated Asians with courtesy. My account does no justice to his really impressive appearance. He had a face carved out of solid Appalachian Mountain rock. Thus it was that when Churchill, seeing Chennault at a Conference, and struck by his appearance, learned of his identity, he remarked sub rosa to his aide: 'Well, thank God he's on our side'. (Quoted by Carton de Wiart, *Happy Odyssey*, Jonathan Cape, 1950, p. 240).

[9] As AGAS had none in stock we got these from OSS. I rather think this is how it came about that an OSS officer later reported supplying Ho with 'six .38 revolvers' at one of his 'several meetings in South China' (*The Lost Revolution*, p. 38). The reminiscences of some of Ho's wartime contacts remind one of the tag Bourrienne ascribed to Napoleon: *C'est l'imagination qui gouverne le genre humain*. (*Life*, ii, 2).

Before leaving Ching Hsi I was warned by the Chinese authorities that most of them are communists, and we ought to know what we are getting ourselves into. But naturally they have to look at things from the Kuomintang point of view.' By now the French were also making a big fuss about our working with Ho and I was called upon by AGAS to furnish a report. When this report was sent to GHQ, we were instructed to continue with the operation regardless.

The first letter I got from Ho reported that OSS had been sending in their own groups who were now co-operating with pro-Vichy Frenchmen, who were more anti-Vietnamese than they were anti-Japanese, so what was the true American policy? This query was impossible to answer, except by admitting its truth.

We had arranged that Ho would send us some of his men for training, which explains the next letter I got from him:

> I will be very much obliged to you of taking care of our boys. I wish they can learn radio and other things necessary in our common fight against the Japs. I hope soon you will be able to visit us here in our base. It will be great! Permit me to send my respect to General Chennault.

These first letters were hand-written with a fine steel pen on thin Chinese rice paper. (An analysis of Ho's handwriting is given in Appendix C.)

Ho's next letter was written on a half sheet of coarse rice paper, faintly lined and coloured pale green.

Dear Mr. Fenn.

Mr. T. & his second get on very well. We become a large family. I hope you'll come to visit us soon.

Sung Minh Fang

Please, be so kind as to give this letter to my friends of the Indo-China café. Ten or 12 days after that, they will hand you a parket; containing allies' flags. I'll be very obliged if you send it to me by the quickest way.

My best greetings to the great old man & to Mr. Bernard & all our friends

I wish you good health & good luck.

Yours sincerely.

June 9. 1945

Hoo

Mr T [Tan] and his second [Mac Sin] get on very well. I hope you'll
come to visit us soon.
Please, be so kind as to give this letter to my friend, Sung Minh
Fang, of the Indochina café. Ten or 12 days after that, they will hand
you a packet containing Allies' flags. I'll be very obliged if you send
it to me by the quickest way. My best greeting to the great old man
[Chennault] and to Mr Bernard and all our friends. I wish you good
health and good luck.

The courier (one of Ho's agents) who brought these letters spoke good
French and we had a long talk. My diary records the substance of the
story he gave me:

Since Ho was away so long there were rumours he had died. Others
said he had gone to America. Then suddenly we heard he had
arrived in Ching Hsi in an American plane. We could hardly believe
it. Then when he arrived at base he had with him this Chinese-
American as well as a radio operator and all sorts of weapons, better
than anything either the French or Japanese had. Uncle Ho arrived
very ill after his long hard walk [the walk Tan had written about],
over two weeks, walking only at night, raining most of the time.
When he got well enough he invited all the top leaders to a conference, not his own people, but rivals working for other groups, who
had used his absence to push themselves forward. Ho told them he
had now secured the help of the Americans including Chennault. At
first nobody really believed him. Then he produced the photograph
of Chennault signed 'Yours sincerely'. After this he sent for the
automatic pistols and gave one to each of the leaders as a present.
The leaders considered Chennault had sent these presents personally.
After this conference there was never any more talk about who was
the top leader.

Soon after, we dropped in a load of supplies; radio sets, medicines,
gadgets, weapons. OSS supplied us with most of this as they had the
bulk of supplies. According to Tan, this drop caused a sensation and
Ho's stock went up another ten points. AGAS wouldn't agree to my
dropping in, so we dropped in a young AGAS officer named Phelan.
He had been reluctant to go on this particular mission because he heard
that Ho was a communist. Within a week of his arrival he was sending
back wires to prove that Ho wasn't in the least a communist: *we* had it
all wrong. For instance one of his wires:

RE DEAL WITH FRENCH YOU ARE MISUNDERSTANDING VIETMINH ATTI-
TUDE THEY NOT ANTI-FRENCH MERELY PATRIOTS DESERVE FULL TRUST
AND SUPPORT.

Robert Shaplen quotes a statement Phelan sent him later, describing
Ho's camp: 'Four huts, each twelve feet square, set four feet off the
ground on bamboo stakes, and Ho's was as bare as the others'.
Amongst other things Phelan mentions that Ho asked his advice about
the opening words of the American Declaration of Independence,
which he wanted to incorporate in his own Declaration. 'But he actually
seemed to know more about it than I did,' says Phelan. Having begun

his mission by grumbling to us that Ho was a communist, Phelan ended his statement to Shaplen by saying, 'He was an awfully sweet guy. If I had to pick out the one quality about that little old man sitting on his hill in the jungle, it was his gentleness.'[10]

Thus it will be seen that these three months since the Jap coup in March 1945 were perhaps the most significant in Ho's career. At the beginning he had been a leader of a party that was but one amongst many: unrecognized by the Americans, opposed by the French, shunned by the Chinese; with no weapons and no equipment. He was also, at the time, cut off from his group by a formidable 600 miles and no chance of flying any part of it. By the end of June, he was, largely thanks to GBT, the unquestioned leader of an overwhelmingly strong revolutionary party. Small wonder that the French, the Chinese and the OSS were now all anxious to utilize this contact.

About this time Gordon returned from America. Dismayed to discover that we were now backing Vietnamese nationalists who were considered anti-French and even pro-Communist, he insisted that Tan should return. Fortunately Tan and Ho between them had already set up an intelligence network of native agents that amply replaced the French net lost by the Japanese coup. This Vietminh net eventually rescued a total of seventeen downed airmen.[11] The Vietminh had also built a landing strip at their headquarters. We were thus able to send in an L-5 to pick up Tan direct. He came back so full of enthusiasm for Ho that Gordon himself became half-converted.[12] Amongst other messages, Tan brought me another letter from Ho, this one typed on an obviously ancient machine, but letter perfect:

> I want to write you a long, long letter to thank you for your friendship. Unfortunately I can't write much, because I am in bad health just now (not very sick, don't worry!).
>
> What I want to say, Mr Tan will say it for me. If you see Messirs Bernard, Vincent, Reiss, and Carlton (of the Information Office) and our other friends, please give them my kindest regards.
>
> Fam said that you will come here. We are ready to give you the heartiest welcome. Do come as soon as you can.

As mentioned earlier, Ho had been very much shaken by his walk in. Tan said he had a bad relapse a month or so later; and shortly before he wrote the above letter, they had even feared for his life. This is confirmed in Vo Nguyen Giap's account:

> For hours he lay in a coma. Every time he came to, he would murmur his thoughts about our work. I refused to believe he was imparting his dying thoughts. But afterwards, looking back on the scene, I realized that he felt so weak that he was dictating his last instructions to me.[13]

---

[10] *The Lost Revolution*, p. 31.
[11] Reported in *Time* magazine, 12 September 1969, but not an official record. Some of these rescues were partly due to other help.
[12] See for example Lacouture *op. cit.*, pp. 74f.
[13] *Days with Ho Chi Minh*, p. 211.

According to Tan he was still quite ill, yet he wished to assure me that he wasn't very sick, that I was not to worry. This awareness of others, despite illness and strain, is also shown in a letter he wrote Tan after the latter's return:

> One thousand excuses: the friend in charge of buying the bracelets for you was sick, he gave that mission to a second person. This person was again sent away to do other job far away from Hanoi. He gave the order of buying to a third person. This latter didn't get it right, and bought only a few of what you wanted. That costs 440p! I send you what they sent me and the balance of 2,560 piastres.
> I wish you good health and good luck. I also wish you to get a good Madame soon.

The bracelets referred to were those made in silver by the tribespeople, which Tan wanted to distribute amongst our staff. We see how much trouble Ho personally went to, even though the errand went amiss. The remark about the 'Madame' is even more significant. Tan (then quite young) was a bachelor, but not through choice. The girl he had been in love with had recently turned him down. It seems he had talked about this to Ho, who revealed that as a young man he himself had been very fond of a girl but when he had gone off to sea (1911) he had had to forget her. After that one time, said Ho, his whole heart seemed to be in the love of his people. But he had sympathized with Tan and even encouraged him to meet some of the girl guerrillas. Unfortunately, said Tan, none of them seemed interested in getting married.

I had one final letter from Ho, dated 'August 1945', written shortly after the dropping of the atom bomb on Hiroshima (6 August):

> The war is finished. It is good for everybody. I feel only sorry that all our American friends have to leave us so soon. And their leaving this country means that relations between you and us will be more difficult.
> The war is won. But we small and subject countries have no share, or very small share, in the victory of freedom and democracy. Probably, if we want to get a sufficient share, we have still to fight. I believe that your sympaty (*sic*) and the sympaty of the great American people will always be with us.
> I also remain sure that sooner or later, we will attain our aim, because it is just. And our country get independent. I am looking forward for the happy day of meeting you and our other American friends either in Indo-China or in the USA!

Fate willed that we should not meet again (see Appendix D, p. 133). With the dropping of the atom bomb and the cessation of hostilities AGAS work in Indo-China was considered finished.

Previous accounts of this particular period in Ho's life, largely coming from OSS sources, have been garbled. Jean Sainteny, de Gaulle's special emissary to Vietnam at this time, and considered one of the best informants on post-war Indo-China, writes:

I often ask myself why OSS, so well endowed with able men, sent into Vietnam only second string underlings, incapable of evaluating the stake and the incalculable results of the drama then taking place in the month of August 1945.[14]

The results for America were unfortunate. Alternately supporting the Vichy-French, Free French, Vietminh and other native groups, OSS managed to infuriate even liberal French opinion while at the same time disillusioning the natives as to any real American understanding. Ho soon realized he could write off that American 'sympaty' he hoped for.[15] It might be argued that this was all to the good: the sooner America disassociated herself from a leading exponent of Marxism the sooner she could get on with defeating world communism. The question to be asked, however, is whether America might have found in Ho not merely a second Tito but a new species of political animal: one who could transmute Marxism into true Internationalism. We shall never know. The chance was lost.

[14] *Histoire d'une Paix Manquée*, Amiot-Dumont, Paris, 1954, p. 95.
[15] See for example *ibid.*, pp. 97 f.

9 Leader

Neither high, nor very far,
Neither emperor, nor king,
You are only a little milestone,
Which stands at the edge of the highway.
To people passing by
You point the right direction,
And stop them from getting lost.
You tell them of the distance
For which they still must journey.
Your service is not a small one.
And people will always remember you.

The fourth ace to be put into Ho's hand was of course the sudden
defeat of Japan. The French had already been eliminated by the
Japanese coup of 9 March. The overthrow of the remaining opponent
left the Vietminh as the only group to operate any kind of effective
government. 'Effective' is perhaps an ironic distortion: the country was
by then totally disrupted. We need only consider the events of the past
five months: the coup of 9 March had in itself abolished the French
administration, which, whatever its limitations, had maintained law and
order and kept the services functioning. Partly to fill the gap and partly
to prevent the French from themselves coming forward to champion
the Vietnamese, the Japanese set up a régime under Bao Dai, a Vietnamese prince of the ancient but largely-obsolete Hué dynasty. By this
move they pretended to offer the Vietnamese self-government. But Bao
Dai had no real following, either amongst the mandarins or the
peasants. Since he was little more than a Japanese puppet (despite an
element of good intention), even his own adherents were likely to prefer
Ho's group to such a régime.

In France, de Gaulle's government had tried to counter this Japanese
move by declaring (24 March) a form of independence for the Vietnamese, who were now to have, amongst other privileges, their own
President. 'Unfortunately they did not make clear what he would
preside over, although they made very clear what he would not preside
over: there was to be a French governor-general who "in the interest of
everyone was to be the arbiter of everything".'[1]

Meanwhile, the running of Indo-China was left largely to the
Japanese army, which had no skill for social, economic and political
affairs. Services broke down, law and order collapsed and bandits
overran both the countryside and towns. Worse still, there was the
threat of famine. The Japanese had for long been exporting rice,
which kept supplies for home consumption at perilously low levels.
Meanwhile, by replacing rice with castor oil beans in order to get oil
supplies, they had seriously cut production. Their final crime against

[1] Henri Azeau, *op. cit.*, p. 37.

native welfare was to neglect the irrigation system; the overflowing rivers had flooded vast areas formerly under cultivation.[2]

At the Potsdam Conference (July 1945) it had been confirmed amongst the Allied Powers that when Japan was defeated, Indo-China, for purposes of occupation, would be divided into two zones. There being no effective French colonial government and the existing French troops being incarcerated, some other Allied forces would have to occupy the country, establish law and order, and disarm the Japanese troops. It was therefore arranged that Chinese forces would take over the north and British forces (from India) the south, with an ultimate return of both areas to France as soon as the above objectives were achieved. As for the Vietnamese, their welfare was to be left in French hands. Truman had modestly substituted Wilson's Fourteen Points with Four Points of his own, which included: 'All peoples who are prepared for self-government should be permitted to chose their own form of government . . . without interference from any foreign source'. Everything depended, of course, on the interpretation of that word 'prepared'. In the case of Vietnam, Malaya and the Dutch East Indies, it was decided that the native populations were not yet 'prepared'.

Students of history will remember that when at Tilsit Napoleon and the Czar Alexander agreed to divide the world between them, their plan was subsequently spoiled by British interference. More than a century later when a similar plan was made at Yalta (and subsequently expanded at Potsdam) British interference was forestalled by offering suitable sops. As things turned out, however, there were other interfering parties, the Chinese, the French, and several clamorous 'emergent nations'.

At that time China and France were considered to make up (along with the US, USSR and UK) the 'big five'; yet France was then defeated, humiliated and largely impotent; while China was backward, disorganized, impoverished and dependent on the US for supplies and armament. France, however, had three points in her favour: first, a vestige of past glory; second, the formidable de Gaulle; and third, her membership in what might be called the Colonial Nations Lobby, consisting of UK, France, Holland and Portugal, who made reciprocal agreements to support one another's colonial claims. The Chinese also had three favourable points: her record of having fought the Japanese longer than any other nation; a government potentially anti-communist (which pleased everyone except the Russians); and the special support of the Americans, who, for complex reasons including missionary propaganda, were sentimentally attached to China. Thus the Chinese were to get back Formosa (Taiwan) and to be allowed the temporary exploitation of North Vietnam; while the French were subsequently to get back all of Indo-China. As for the emergent nations, they could only hope to get a slice of the cake by either having already exacted agreements towards independence or by immediate national resistance.

We have seen how, following the Japanese coup in March and the setting up of the puppet government under Bao Dai, de Gaulle had felt constrained to offer a quick counter-proposal of Vietnamese independence. The terms set out did indeed suggest more independence than

[2] It was later estimated that a million Vietnamese died from these devastations during 1945/6. See *The Lost Revolution*, p. 43.

the natives had formerly enjoyed. But there was still this French governor-general 'upon whom, for the benefit of everybody, the final responsibility would lie.' Ho would naturally have wondered how his countrymen were likely to benefit from a French governor-general. But worse still was the French intention to keep Indo-China divided into the former five regions: not only were Laos and Cambodia to be separated, which might have been accepted, but the three divisions of Tonkin, Annam, and Cochin China were also to be kept. Ho naturally rejected this proposal out of hand.

At this time however (July 1945) hardly anyone yet took heed of Ho: and least of all France. De Gaulle sent off his emissary, Jean Sainteny, to contact the 'most suitable native group' with whom to discuss and implement the new proposals. Sainteny went down to Ching Hsi for discussions with the Dong Minh Hoi set up by Chang Fa-kwei the previous year. Sainteny, being a man of discernment, soon found out that the only group with any real following inside Indo-China was the Vietminh, with a leader named Ho whom the French had scarcely heard of. (Nguyen Ai Quoc, long known to the French *Sûreté* as a Comintern agent, was officially dead, and nobody had yet connected He Who Enlightens with Nguyen the Patriot.) Sainteny tried to get in touch with Ho; but as the only existing communication was through our GBT radio in Kunming, he failed to do so. Furthermore he was unable to persuade either the American Air Force or the OSS to fly him inside.[2a]

While he was thus hamstrung, the two atom bombs were dropped. Ho seized this moment of general stupefaction to call for the general uprising that his associates had been urging on him for so long but for which he had previously thought the moment unpropitious. On 15 August the Japanese surrendered and the following day handed over the reins of government to Bao Dai and his group. But already Giap's spearhead of Vietminh forces was entering Hanoi, and replacing the red and yellow imperial flags with the gold star on red of the Vietminh. By the 20th of the month Giap was in effective control of the city; and five days later (a mere ten days after Japanese surrender) the Vietminh were putting up their flags everywhere in North Vietnam.[3]

On the same day (25 August) Bao Dai announced in a public declaration that 'we have decided to abdicate and we transfer power to the democratic Republican Government.' He expressed three wishes:

[2a] Sainteny took great umbrage at this, particularly later on in Hanoi when he found amongst some papers OSS had left behind a telegram that read 'In no circumstances must the French get inside Indo-China'. (*Histoire d'une Paix Manquée*, p. 95). In this respect he did OSS something of an injustice. What had happened was that OSS wanted to drop certain Frenchmen into Ho's camp and they asked GBT to get clearance. Ho suspected these Frenchmen of being anti-Vietminh and Tan wired us that if any Frenchmen were dropped into the Vietminh camp they would be arrested and clapped in gaol. So it was our GBT message, duly relayed by OSS Kunming, that Sainteny found. But the Frenchmen were dropped in despite our warning and promptly arrested. They included Pierre Messmer, now (autumn 1972) Prime Minister of France.

[3] Philippe Devillers, *Histoire du Vietnam*, p. 142.

1. We request that the new government should take care of dynastic temples and royal tombs.
2. We request that the new government should deal fraternally with all parties and groups which have fought for the independence of our country even though they have not closely followed the popular movement; to do this in order to give them the opportunity to participate in the reconstruction of the country and to demonstrate that the new régime is built upon the absolute union of the entire population.
3. We invite all parties and groups, all classes of society, as well as the royal family, to solidarize in unreserved support of the democratic government with a view to consolidating the national independence.[4]

But Ho eliminated all nationalist parties!!

During all this period Ho had been directing affairs from the Vietminh headquarters in Tuyen Quang, some 50 miles northwest of Hanoi. The appeal of 10 August calling for a general uprising had been signed Nguyen Ai Quoc. This was probably in order to make a wide appeal to all those compatriots from north to south to whom this name had for decades been a rallying cry. Most of these had long supposed Nguyen Ai Quoc was dead; and this surprising re-emergence was a powerful tocsin. As for the French, they were *certain* he was dead. At first they assumed some other dissident had used the name. But when the *Sûreté* got hold of a photograph, the astute Arnoux (see p. 34) at once knew who it was. 'Faute d'empreintes digitales, c'est à l'oreille que nous identifions les gens. Il n'y avait pas à s'y tromper. C'etait bien là celle de ce Nguyen Ai Quoc.'[5]

Communist!!

In regard to the Vietnamese population, only those inside the Vietminh inner circle knew that Nguyen Ai Quoc was now called Ho. When the leader had to present himself as a public figure it was necessary to establish his identity. There was obviously no further need for pseudonyms: the revolutionaries (that is, the Vietminh) were now the government. It would have been pointless, after thirty years, for Ho to return to his original name. The question was: which of his pseudonyms should he take? The choice might have seemed to rest on Nguyen Ai Quoc – most famous of those pseudonyms. But perhaps at this point Ho felt it was better not to take up a name so entirely associated with rebellion. He needed now to establish himself as a different sort of patriot: one who would consolidate rather than rebel. Under this name of Ho Chi Minh he knew himself to be tolerated by the Chinese, accepted by the Americans, and at least not proscribed by the French. As for his own countrymen: they needed only to be told the name of the liberator to begin cheering.

It was not, however, until 29 August that the new government

---

[4] For full text of this abdication see *Vietnam, History, Documents and Opinions*, pp. 66–7.
[5] 'Failing finger prints, it's by the ears we identify people. We couldn't be mistaken. This was certainly Nguyen Ai Quoc'. Quoted by Lacouture, *Cinq Hommes et la France*, Editions du Seuil, Paris 1961, p. 13. Ho's ears, indeed, were particularly distinctive, the right one being almost elfin.

fficially announced its composition and the identity of its leader. Ho was presented as 'a national patriot who had devoted his whole life to achieving his country's independence'. In less than a week nearly the whole population was referring to him affectionately as 'Uncle'.

While these events were transforming the country, the French were excluded from taking part. Sainteny, fuming on the Chinese border, had to wait until 22 August before OSS flew him into Hanoi: two whole days after Giap had taken control of the city. Five more days went by before he was able to meet the Vietminh commander. At this point Sainteny had some small revenge (if one may call it that) for the humiliations he and all France had endured in the past weeks: he was able to tell Giap that his triumph was short-lived; any day now the Chinese troops would enter Vietnam and take over the whole of the North, while the British would simultaneously take over the South.[6] This news for Giap was a shock; for Ho it spelled disaster. It was as if Fate, having dealt him those four aces, had now at one blow knocked all the cards from his hand. As far as Ho was concerned, the British were as bad as the French but the Chinese were worse.[7] The French and British behaved according to a pattern. Even the Japanese had been a *controlled* force. Ho knew that the behaviour of the Chinese forces would be both unpredictable and licentious. This was not so much because of their being Chinese as because of their being Kuomintang. Led by a predatory Yunnanese warlord, Lu Han, for whom this expedition would be only an excuse for plunder, they could easily transform the present disruption of the country into total anarchy.

At this point the French might certainly have come to terms with the Vietminh on more favourable conditions than were ever to be exacted later. Ho saw that he would need French support in dealing with these Chinese predators;[8] and with his usual Hochiminity would have worked out a deal to give the French not only the economic concessions they were after but also the aura of *La Gloire* that went with keeping Indo-China inside the French Union. But it seemed that apart from Sainteny, the French hierarchy were determined to prevent an understanding. Even General Leclerc (Commander of the French forces designated to take over from the Chinese and British), who was basically liberal, declaimed with chauvinistic fervour that France would uphold her rights in Indo-China 'with force, if force were necessary'; while Admiral d'Argenlieu, who was to be appointed High Commissioner, spouted

But Ho applied Mao Ste Tung's program to govern Vietnam!!

[6] The Potsdam Conference, see p. 86.

[7] 'Vietnamese feelings towards the Chinese are not unlike those of the Irish for the English of Oliver Cromwell's day. When the Chinese troops occupied North Vietnam for a few months after World War II, their behaviour justified all Vietnamese fears, for they pillaged, stole, cheated and took with them from the country everything of value that was movable.' P. J. Honey, *Communism in North Vietnam*, M.I.T. Press, 1963, p. 3.

[8] 'The uncompromising and incorruptible revolutionary *à la Saint Just*, tempered by twenty years of clandestine exile while struggling against the French, was willing to compromise with us only to eliminate the Yunnanese invaders.' Paul Mus, *Vietnam, Sociologie d'une Guerre*, Editions du Seuil. Paris 1952. p. 88.

about 'France's greatness, that would not permit the anarchy of native revolution'. Certainly Ho's *Declaration of Independence*, proclaimed to the surging Hanoi throngs on 2 September, did not show any diminution of anti-French bitterness. The list of French 'crimes' against the Vietnamese people fills a whole page. It is this document[9] that Ho begins with the opening words of an even more historic document, the American Declaration of Independence: 'All men are created equal. They are endowed by their Creator with certain inalienable[10] rights, among these are Life, Liberty and the pursuit of Happiness.'

Did his thoughts go back to that day thirty-three years earlier when he had discovered an America where yellow people walked the streets freely? Yet within a decade the America he admired would become his enemy.

Meanwhile thousands of Japanese soldiers still carrying their arms stood around the Hanoi streets in dazed apathy, varied here and there with a resentment they could scarcely hide, considering the trick that fate had played them. For five long years they had been the victorious occupiers, with never a rebuff. Now they were to be disarmed by the despised Chinese whom they or their countrymen had previously overcome in almost every battle. It was indeed a bitter pill. Yet somehow they did in the end swallow it with a resignation that might even have been admired had they not been so unloved. Staying well out of their way were groups of Frenchmen, recently released from gaol and still conspicuously unarmed. They were perhaps even more dazed than the Japs. There were almost no incidents. Even after the Vietminh had emptied the prisons (mostly full of political prisoners) law and order continued to reign.

Immediately after proclaiming independence Ho set to work on practical matters. The most urgent task was to offset the devastating effects of the famine. Plans were made for intensive cultivation; quick-growing crops were sown. Fast-days and rationing were introduced. The use of grain for liquor distillation was banned. Hoarding was made subject to severe penalties. But despite such measures, hundreds of thousands died in these weeks that were among the most glorious and terrible in Vietnamese history.

Terrible not only because of the famine but because of the Chinese troops who had now arrived. The occupation was even worse than Ho feared: the arrangement had been largely a concession by the Allies to Chiang Kai-shek for his contribution to the war effort. It was therefore accepted by him as a chance for exploitation. Chiang had passed on this lucky dip to one of his most rapacious warlords, General Lu Han of Yunnan, whose troops looted as they pleased and merely in the process of living off the land cut further into the already inadequate food supplies. Meanwhile, Lu Han's inner circle collected arms from the Japanese (which they sold to the Vietnamese), imposed Chinese currency at ten times its value, and finally charged $23m. 'to cover costs'. Ho found himself combating not only an economic breakdown but a

---

[9] For complete text, see *Vietnam, History, Documents and Opinions*, pp. 64–6.
[10] This appears to be the actual spelling Ho used in his English version. Wherever he took it from, it was not from the *Encyclopedia Americana* (see p. 76) which correctly quotes the original spelling of 'unalienable'.

disruptive occupying army, worse than the French, and worse than the Japanese, since not even those exploiters could afford to be totally indifferent to the population.

It was because Ho had to get rid of these locusts that he needed to come to terms with the French: they in turn were equally desperate to get rid of the invaders. Since the fall of France five years earlier, she had been subjected to a mounting barrage of insults from a nation she had formerly insulted freely. Now when the Chinese occupied this area that the French had snatched from their sphere of influence only eighty years earlier they showed their spleen by holding the 3,500 French troops in Hanoi semi-prisoners, ringing de Gaulle's delegates with armed guards and ordering the tricolor to be taken down. As a final humiliation they hung up Vietminh flags with their own and even marched arm in arm along the Hanoi streets with Giap's guerrillas. Although Ho himself was never taken in by these demonstrations of 'Asiatic kinship', the French were none the less shaken by this evidence of an anti-white front. They need scarcely have worried: for the reasons we have stated Ho had no desire to form an Asiatic bloc.

Meanwhile a very different sort of occupation – unpredatory, well-disciplined, almost high minded, yet in one respect even more questionable – had taken place down south. As we have noted, this occupation had been given over to the British. The instructions to the occupying troops were those agreed at Potsdam: restore law and order; disarm and repatriate the Japanese troops. The Chinese had left 'law and order' to the Vietminh, finding them adequate to deal with it. They had attended to the second requirement with reasonable despatch. In the South it was a very different story. The British interest in law and order plus disarming the Japanese came second to the requirements of their secret agreement to re-instate the French. Finding the Vietminh in control of Saigon, Major-General Douglas Gracey, the commander of the British occupying forces, at once set about re-arming the French troops recently let out of gaol and utilising them to re-inforce his own troops in a vigorous campaign to smash the Vietminh. Not wholly succeeding in this onslaught he then enlisted the support of the Japanese commander General Terauchi, who was so ready to lend his own troops that he subsequently received 'the highest praise' for his co-operation. 'The British were delighted with the discipline shown by the late enemy and were often warmly admiring, in the best playing-field tradition, of their fine military qualities.'[11]

With the use of the Japanese troops the British were able to hold the fort until General Leclerc took over with his own 50,000 troops. General Gracey has not been without his staunch supporters in thus helping to stem international communism.[12] But it would be difficult for anybody who knows at first hand the Japanese atrocities in World War II to read of his collaboration without a qualm.

[11] Harold Isaacs, quoted in *Vietnam, History, Documents and Opinions*, p. 49. Isaacs was an eye-witness of these events. See also, Edgar Snow, *The Other Side of the River*, Gollancz, 1963, Philippe Devillers, *Histoire du Vietnam Nord*, 1945–51, Editions du Seuil, Paris 1952, and Earl Mountbatten in Section E of Report to Combined Chiefs of Staff, H.M.S.O., 1969.
[12] See for example Alyn Glyn, *Witness to Vietnam*, Johnson, 1968, pp. 31/2.

This instance of politics making strange bedfellows was echoed from the political left with an equally sinister example: the French military re-occupation of the south, initiated in chicanery and consolidated in blood, was promoted by a government in which the dominant party was actually communist and thus might have been expected to support the colonial freedom movement rather than suppress it. In the North the French had shown a certain awareness of native aspirations; in the South they not only lacked such awareness but behaved with the old chauvinistic ruthlessness.

We have seen that from the outset Ho was never wholly in sympathy with the French Communist Party, whom he considered to have neglected colonial problems. In 1945 his relationship further deteriorated. Maurice Thorez, Party chief at the time (and actually Deputy Premier of France) is reported to have said, 'We cannot trust Ho – he is a Trotskyist at heart.'[13] This remark stemmed largely from that period in 1935 when the newly-formed Indo-Chinese Communist Party was accused by the FCP of having 'flirted' with the Trotskyites in Indo-China. But it was the sort of remark Ho could easily brush off. More serious was Thorez's widely-circulated statement that he 'ardently hoped to see the French flag flying over every territory in the French Union and had not the slightest intention of being held responsible for a sell-out of France's positions in Indo-China'.[14] This was possibly inspired by Soviet pressure: Moscow felt that if France was going Communist (which then seemed likely) it was better to keep her colonies inside the European Communist hierarchy than to let them wander off into Asiatic independence. Whatever the inspiration for Thorez's attitude, Ho disliked it.

It was at this same time that the Indo-Chinese Communist Party was disbanded, to be shortly substituted by 'Marxist study groups', and then, in 1951, by the Workers' Party (Lao Dong) (see p. 106). Various explanations have been offered for the disbandment, including the above friction with the FCP. Another reason given is that this was one further step in Ho's policy, initiated with the forming of the Vietminh, of appearing as a genuine nationalist rather than as an international communist. Ho had a particular reason to veil his communism at this time: Chiang Kai-shek was now girding himself for a decisive struggle with the Red Army; and for Ho to continue as the head of a declared communist state was to invite a permanent take-over from Chiang's occupying troops. By disbanding the ICP Ho rejected any open association with the Chinese Communists.[15]

But was Ho's move a voluntary gesture or was it a price demanded by Chiang? And why did Ho never again re-instigate the ICP as such instead of continuing to call it 'the Workers' Party'? Perhaps he felt that this gave him some small reason to escape allegiance to Moscow; he may have foreseen the danger of being head of a State subservient to the

---

13 Quoted in *The Lost Revolution*, p. 40.
14 Quoted by Lacouture, *Ho Chi Minh*, p. 121. And Ellen Hammer in *The Struggle for Indochina* (Institute of Pacific Relations, Stanford University Press, 1954), p. 190 quotes *l'Humanité*, 24 July 1946, to the same effect.
15 See Frank N. Trager (ed.), *Marxism in Southeast Asia*, Stanford University Press, 1959, p. 155.

Comintern. We observe that it was *after* Communist China was able to declare itself a full reality (October 1949) that Ho established the Workers' Party (February 1951); almost as if he anticipated the problems that would later harass fully-declared Communist Parties throughout the world in their relations with the USSR. At the same time, North Vietnam has never become a satellite of China.[16]

As to what the USSR thought about the move,[17] Ho may have been disinclined to care. During this period, indeed, Moscow gave him not even verbal support. Ho was thus left isolated by both Left and Right. The Russian negligence may have been nothing more than pre-occupation with more overwhelming problems; but it was likely to have been intentional. At this period the Russians had a clear understanding with de Gaulle. When in 1943 he had been brushed off by the British and Americans, he had turned for help to Stalin who had then given it on the understanding that de Gaulle would back Soviet post-war claims and vice versa. Thus it came about that whatever France wanted with regard to Indo-China received prior consideration over whatever the Indo-Chinese themselves might want. After all – 'how many divisions had *they* got?'[18]

In Hanoi, therefore, Ho found himself threatened by the following combination of adverse circumstances: General Leclerc's 50,000 troops in the South ready to come North for an all-out war of suppression; the occupying Chinese who had no intention of leaving while there was still blood to be drawn; and a clamorous rivalry of political enemies amongst his own countrymen, ready to exploit Ho's every weakness.[19]

'Judge a woman by her lovers but a man by his friends': it is not without significance that amongst all the Frenchmen with whom Ho had contact during these tight-rope years, Sainteny is the one he trusted and liked best. It was certainly not the fault of Sainteny that Franco-Vietnamese relations inexorably spun downwards into the final shambles of Dien Bien Phu. If we examine the struggles of this untiring negotiator, whether in his own book, *Histoire d'une Paix Manquée*, or in the comments of his associates and others (such as Paul Mus, Philippe Devillers, Jean Lacouture, Bernard Fall, Harold Isaacs and Robert Shaplen) we find a Frenchman who might well be awarded the palm not only for intelligence and perseverance, but for modesty and

[handwritten margin note: Ho has been always a Stalinist (since 1925)]

[16] The US seems to have always assumed (although with increasing uncertainty) that Ho operated at the dictates of the USSR and China, more particularly of the former. Certainly he depended heavily on the support of these two powers; but the nearest he ever came to accepting their dictates would appear to have been at the Geneva Conference, and in this case their dictates coincided with the dictates of Ho's personal insight (see p. 111). This US misconception of Ho's actual independence led them to waste endless time and effort on persuading Moscow to bring the war to an end.

[17] See McLane, *op. cit.*, p. 433, and other pertinent comments, pp. 267 f.

[18] Within only five years they did indeed have enough divisions to get their names on Stalin's list. Nevertheless, it was not until the newly-emerged Chinese People's Republic recognized Ho's régime (1950) that the USSR were shamed into following suit a week or so later.

[19] See, for example, Paul Mus, *Vietnam, Sociologie d'une Guerre*, p. 74.

human understanding. Men of calibre seek each other out. And here is Sainteny's own estimate of Ho:

> In order to achieve his aims, Ho Chi Minh is always able to be less exacting than his rivals . . . to be satisfied with relative independence, trusting to French honour that after a certain period complete independence will be granted to his country. In this, Ho was certainly sincere.[20] He had struggled towards this end for 35 years; he could certainly wait a few years more.
>
> His wide culture, his intelligence, his unbelievable activity, his asceticism and his total disinterestedness lent him in the eyes of the population an incomparable prestige and popularity. It is certainly regrettable that France undervalued this man and was unable to assess his value and the power he wielded. His proposals, his deeds, his attitude, his approach (whether intimate or formal), everything conduced towards proving that he loathed a solution by force. There's no doubt that he aspired during the whole of this time to become the Gandhi of Indo-China.[21]

It took Ho and Sainteny (aided by Leclerc, General Salan and Jean Pignon)[22] five months to arrive at a settlement. Within his own party Ho had to contend with opposition both from the Right and the Left, as well as from Bao Dai representing neither. The right wing were obstructionist for various reasons: some were pro-Chinese, some pro-French and some merely pro-themselves. The left wing were against any kind of settlement, which they insisted could only be a sell-out to the French, however reasonable. Bao Dai, surprisingly enough, took much the same line: he apparently felt he must now establish his complete disassociation from the French.

Sainteny also had to contend with a mixed entourage: in sympathy with the *idée-fixe* relic of the colonial régime, who thought that any Vietminh triumph was an effrontery, was the High Commissioner, Admiral Thierry d'Argenlieu, one of France's unhappier choices at a time when the wind of change might well have been called a gale. Sainteny also found himself opposed by a left wing of younger men who wanted to give even more independence than Ho was willing to settle for. Leclerc himself, who with his army seemed in the best position to be recalcitrant, was fortunately a realist at heart: he not only saw the limitations of that army (totally deprived of help from France, since there were neither supplies to send nor transport to send them in) he also saw the menace of the Chinese troops whose temporary occupational role was, as we have indicated, threatening to become a permanent one.

The terms that Ho and Sainteny hammered out had to give consideration to all these conflicting elements. But the main point at issue was how much 'independence' Vietnam was to be allowed – and how much sovereignty France was to retain. It was thus February 1946

---

[20] Confirmed by McLane (*op. cit.*, p. 272) who states 'There is no need to doubt that these public pronouncements . . . were genuine.'

[21] *Histoire d'une Paix Manquée*, p. 166.

[22] The last two respectively, military consultant and political adviser.

before an agreement was reached. As for the Chinese, France bought
them off by giving up all her concessions in China as well as her lease
in far-north Kwangchowan and her stake in the railway line running up
to Kunming. Ho in turn had to agree to take into his government a
large element of pro-Chinese officials and make special customs concessions. Whose pill was the more bitter to swallow? But the one thing
Ho and Sainteny were fully united about was that the Chinese must be
got rid of at almost any price.

Under the terms of this hard-fought agreement, France recognized
the Republic of Vietnam as a free state, but one remaining inside the
French Union and forming part of the Indo-Chinese Federation. To be
'inside the French Union' was barely acceptable; but to form 'a part of
the Indo-Chinese Federation' was one of the two most astringent
ingredients of Ho's particular medicine. It was tantamount to recognizing Cochin China, i.e. South Vietnam, as a separate area. France
sweetened the dose by promising a referendum that would allow the
South Vietnamese to make their own choice as to whether they wanted
to unify with the north. The other odious ingredient Ho knew to be
inevitable: the French army must be allowed entry in order to ensure
that the Chinese army went out. This was the international arrangement
that Chiang had agreed to and could not evade without open renuncia-
tion of an international obligation. In regard to the measures for
effecting genuine and total evacuation of Chinese troops the French
made their own arrangements.

But Ho also took careful precaution that the Chinese would really
keep to the bargain by having the pro-Chinese leader of the VNQDD,
Vu Hong Khanh, also a signatory to the treaty. This not only constituted a sort of guarantee that Chiang would stick to the terms but
precluded any later criticisms that Ho himself had utilized the French
to get rid of the Chinese.

This agreement that had been fought over for six months in an
atmosphere of hate, distrust and imminent carnage, was finally signed
(6 March 1946) amidst the jingle of champagne glasses. Ho knew how
to accept the inevitability of ceremony as well as of compromise. The
spectre at the feast was Giap, whose sister had died in a French prison
and his wife on a French scaffold. But Giap was willing at this point
to hide his Francophobia; and it was indeed he who announced to the
Hanoi throng a treaty he openly compared with Brest-Litovsk.[23]

[23] At which (March 1918) Lenin secured 'a breathing space' from the Germans
at the cost of drastic concessions.

10 Warrior

The ancients used to like to sing about natural beauty:
Snow and flowers, moon and wind, mists, mountains and rivers.
Today we should make poems including iron and steel,
And the poet also should know how to lead an attack.

Amongst the Vietnamese generally this agreement not only to permit separation of the South but to invite back the hated French troops was received with fury and alarm. Confidence in Uncle Ho was badly shaken. He had to plead desperately: 'Fellow countrymen who have followed me up to now, follow me once more. I would prefer death a hundred times to betraying my country.'[1]

Only those inside the hierarchy could understand what dire necessity had driven their leader to such concessions. It was unlikely that Ho really 'trusted in French honour', as Sainteny suggested; he merely trusted more in Leclerc than in Lu Han. He was probably right in his decision. But Giap was also right in trusting neither.

France blundered into her disastrous war more through misjudgement than through bad intentions. For a few weeks the diplomatic wheels were kept greased by Ho and Sainteny. Leclerc also showed himself able to accept the new relationship in a fashion that would later put to shame his less forward-looking colleagues. The French troops entered North Vietnam with almost no incidents. Leclerc happily stipulated that two-thirds of his personal escort should be Vietminh veterans.

D'Argenlieu, however, remained intransigent. Since he would neither go to Hanoi himself, nor welcome in Saigon a man he had recently considered a rebel deserving instant execution, it was arranged that Ho, accompanied by Sainteny, should meet him on board a French cruiser in the Bay of Along. There is a splendid photograph of Ho in a sun-helmet, sitting with Sainteny inside the Catalina flying-boat that took them to this meeting. Ho, tight lipped and unsmiling, seems essentially the old revolutionary instead of the new Uncle Ho. Another photograph shows the pair now on board the cruiser, with d'Argenlieu trying to look gracious.

Meanwhile Giap was meeting other Frenchmen in Dalat, Saigon's famous hill station. The indomitable military leader soon discovered a new cause of complaint against the French: it appeared that the referendum in South Vietnam (which the Vietminh were almost certain to win) was now subject to ratification by the French Parliament. This decision was based upon the legal status of Cochin China within the Indo-Chinese Federation. All this was mere humbug to Giap. His bitter reports widened the breech.

One of the terms of the agreement of 6 March 1946 was that the ratification (to include various unresolved points) would be later made

[1] Quoted in *The Lost Revolution*, p. 40.

in Paris. Pham Van Dong was appointed to be head of the Vietminh delegation. It was obviously right that the Foreign Minister should conduct the negotiations. But how could the Vietminh – how indeed could the French? – pull this final rabbit out of the hat without the presence of the master magician? So Ho was to go along later.

The delegation left for Paris in April 1946. It so happened that I myself was in the city at that time and met Pham Van Dong and his associates casually on the steps of the Sorbonne. I had lost touch with Indo-Chinese affairs and did not know of Pham's ministerial post. He and his team seemed so young and unassuming that I took them to be junior staff.[2] I remember only one thing of significance that we talked about: someone said it wouldn't be too difficult to reach an agreement in Paris; the hard part would come later in making that agreement stick in Vietnam. Paris might mean what they said, but Frenchmen *là-bas* intended to go their own way. This remark was certainly prophetic. It must have been only a week or two later that d'Argenlieu, having waited for Ho to be safely out of the country, proclaimed the 'Republic of Cochin China' as a completely free state.

After this *volte-face* there was a second shock: Ho's plane, instead of taking him to Paris, set him down in Biarritz. The reason given for this was that while he was en route the French elections had put a new government in power; and not until this was properly in the saddle could negotiations start.

Sainteny met Ho at the airfield and explained this curious twist. It says much for the trust and understanding between these two men that before Paris was ready to receive him, Ho stayed three weeks in Biarritz. Was it only Sainteny's persuasive powers that kept him there when he could so easily have boarded a plane and flown home? Here was another instance of Hochiminity: having decided that he *must* get the treaty ratified he made the best of his enforced stay not only by enjoying himself but by endearing himself to the French population. He wandered around the town and countryside almost like a tourist, getting to know both the sailors and the peasants, taking boat rides, even visiting Lourdes. Sainteny writes about 'his personality at once fatherly and gay: Uncle Ho, who loved to gather the children round him for a family photograph, to chat with French peasants along the country roads, to visit the sick and wounded in the Lanessan hospital.'[3] It's almost as if Ho took a holiday, only the second one in his life (the first being that period in Sochi). Although this holiday was forced upon him, where could he be happier than in France, his second home? And how ironic that, after such a life, fate should have landed him here in Biarritz, favourite resort of emperors! Although Ho had recently been elevated to the Presidency, which should have offered a degree of comfort, conditions in post-war Vietnam were still very grim. Furthermore, Ho had chosen to live in an out-building. Here in Biarritz, he was quartered in the Hôtel du Palais (generally considered the best); and Biarritz is (or was) a town that manages to combine charm with luxury. One of the more ridiculous sidelights of this curious episode is that

---

[2] Amongst the half-dozen present were (in addition to Dong) Tran Duc Thao, Le Duc Tho and Xuan Thuy, all to become key men subsequently.
[3] *Histoire d'une Paix Manquée*, p. 167.

various members of the government who were communists (and on that account no doubt felt themselves particularly concerned for his welfare) came here to visit the distinguished guest, and made a fuss not because the President had been sidetracked from his purpose (on which the fate of Vietnam, and even France, was to lie) but because he had been put into a 'second-class hotel undergoing repair'.[4]

At last, on the 22 June, Sainteny got clearance to take Ho to Paris. According to the Frenchman's account, Ho was overwhelmed by the huge crowds ringing the field at Le Bourget. And as the plane came to a halt on the runway, he clutched Sainteny's shoulder and exclaimed, 'Surtout, ne me quittez pas, il y a tant de monde'.[5] Sainteny, essentially a serious man (as his photographs reveal) took this remark seriously; but I rather think that Ho, who had undergone more perils than a Hollywood superspy, would have scarcely been concerned about a crowd of Frenchmen, even though he had been execrating them for thirty years. Ironically, amongst those Frenchmen, the chief government representative was Marius Moutet, one of Ho's communist cronies from the early Paris days, now Minister for Overseas Territories. Ho had previously come to Paris unknown and penniless. Now he was accommodated at the Royal Monceau, one of the five or six top hotels in this queen city of *hôtels de luxe*. Here old friends and new flocked to greet him; Ho's suite became an embassy. As always he made a hit with everyone. The French are exactly the nation to understand and appreciate Hochiminity. They love to make contact, delight in talk, enjoy individuality and above all appreciate intelligence and what Sainteny calls Ho's *'vaste culture'*. In her long history Paris has taken to her heart innumerable celebrities; but perhaps there has never been one who achieved more spontaneous popularity. Upon his arrival he was still only a name in the newspapers; upon leaving he was almost as much Uncle Ho in France as in Vietnam. Shaplen describes the scene:

> Ho enjoyed a huge success, he charmed everyone. He was widely compared to Confucius, to the Buddha, to St John the Baptist. Everywhere he went, whether to the opera, to a fancy reception, to a picnic or to a press conference, he appeared in his simple, high-buttoned linen work suit. His wit, his oriental courtesy, his *savoir-faire*, his mixed profundity and playfulness in social intercourse, his open love for children, above all his sincerity and simplicity, captured one and all.
>
> 'Moscow is heroic, but Paris is the joy of living,' said Ho. 'What a wonderful city, what a wonderful scene!'[6]

Amongst the numerous photographs of this Francophile is one showing him at a sort of picnic in the grounds of Versailles. He is sitting on the grass verge with a family of French *élite*, all of them, including the child, dressed up to the nines; Ho too looks suave, groomed, almost dapper, as though he himself has absorbed something of France.

---

[4] Lacouture, *op. cit.*, p. 116 and others.
[5] 'Don't on any account leave me, there are so many people here.' *Histoire d'une Paix Manquée*, p. 203.
[6] *The Lost Revolution*, pp. 47/8.

But behind this façade of bonhomie (genuine though it was) lay a structure both complex and fragile. The Vietnamese people were demanding independence and unity. In regard to independence the French were determined to grant them only that measure of it which accorded with their concepts of the 'Indo-Chinese Federation' and the 'French Union': both elastic terms; and in regard to unity France was equally determined to keep Cochin China as a separate unit. This concept was anathema to Ho. As we have emphasized, Cochin China was ethnically, culturally and historically tied to the rest of Vietnam. It was also vital to the whole. The French wanted to keep it separate and under their control because it was the richest part of Indo-China, with the largest rice fields and rubber plantations, sizeable cotton, coffee, spice and other products, and significant mines, including gold. Saigon, too, was a thriving industrial city as well as an international port. Three-fifths of all French investment in Indo-China was thus centred in Cochin China. The Indo-Chinese Federation was also an excuse for the French to retain their influence in Laos and Cambodia. While not insisting that these areas should be attached to Vietnam, Ho was anxious they should stay free from France.

But the greatest weakness in the structure was the composition of the French government. At this crucial period, a peculiar combination of communists, socialists and opportunist 'liberals' were working together under Bidault in an atmosphere of suspicion and hostility. No further comment need be offered about the attitude of Bidault and his government than this report from his chief of protocol, Jacques Dumaine:

> Ho's landing at Le Bourget developed into a real crisis – anything could have happened. Ho Chi Minh is evidently playing the rôle of Mahatma although his simplicity seems to be genuine. He carries on with his pointless visit to France although he is doubtless worrying about what might be happening in his Vietnam; however, he does not want to go back there with nothing to show. On July 14th he caused me a further headache when the question of his official place at the march-past cropped up. M. Bidault did not want him anywhere near but Uncle Ho insisted on being placed close to him so that I had to work out the position of Ho's seat in the official stand to the nearest centimetre.[7]

Ho now for the first time had an opportunity to assess the value of his French Communist friends. While never quarrelling with any of them, he quietly noted that they knew almost nothing about Far-eastern affairs. Thorez's main concern about Indo-China was that in line with Stalin's hegemony: a Communist France would still keep the tricolor flying over Indo-China as well as every other territory in the French Union. Thus Ho got no help from the Communists in these negotiations at Fontainebleau. Worse still, he soon discovered that the French government had sent as delegates only second-stringers. At this time (1946) the Colonial Powers were still living, as far as Asia was concerned, in a world dated 1910. The French politicians still treated their Vietnamese opposite numbers with patronage that even made fun of

---

[7] *Quai d'Orsay*, Chapman & Hall, 1958, pp. 63/4.

'these little men, ill-kempt, inexperienced, essentially naïve'. There was perhaps some basis for thinking them naïve: although Ho did not really trust the French he still had to trust 'international law', which nations instigated for their general convenience and therefore might be supposed to conform to. Ho was similarly unlucky at Geneva eight years later.[8] In international law, when large countries sign they get ready for the worst: when small countries sign they must hope for the best.

But d'Argenlieu's coup in Cochin China killed the Fontainebleau Conference before it even got started. Ho struggled to get some sort of assurance that the South would not be irremediably detached. He knew that to go home without such an assurance would leave him impossibly weakened *vis-à-vis* his colleagues in Hanoi. There were many of them (including Giap), who had never believed the talks were anything but a French trick to gain time while they consolidated their military strength. The best that Ho could get (14 September) was a *modus vivendi* (signed, ironically enough, by Marius Moutet), offering little more than an understanding about some *future* settlement. Ho had been in the position of a man who must sell his watch to the pawnbroker for whatever he can get.

A few days later he set sail for home on board a French sloop. Why did he waste a further month on a sea voyage instead of taking a three-day flight by plane? According to Sainteny, Ho feared an 'accident': only a few days earlier Tai Li, head of the Chinese secret police, had been killed in a plane accident whose origin suggested a coup. Unless Ho had received a very definite warning of a similar 'accident' it seems unlikely that this consideration would have weighed: he had faced possible assassination too many times before. Nor does it seem likely that he sought the slow route home merely to put off an unpleasant meeting with his colleagues. Perhaps he felt exhausted by his three months of night-and-day activity in Paris. We hear from the captain of the sloop that despite the near-failure of his mission Ho was in top form during the whole voyage and 'proved the liveliest of table companions'.[9]

But a new twist was in store. On Ho's arrival d'Argenlieu agreed to meet him off the South Vietnam coast, on board the cruiser *Suffren*. A group of journalists had also been invited. Ho informed them that the Fontainebleau Conference was to be implemented in Vietnam by another conference in January; and would the journalists help to improve relations by reporting this demonstration of Franco-Vietnamese solidarity? Lacouture (who was present) says that Ho then turned to embrace the High Commissioner. 'The look on the Admiral's face at that moment had to be seen to be believed.'[10]

During the next several weeks Franco-Vietnamese relationships rocked along in uneasy watchfulness and mutual distrust. The Vietminh in the South tried not to provoke incidents that would give the French any further excuse to postpone the promised referendum. In the North Giap went on preparing for D-Day.

Early in November the French let it out that they were opening a

[8] See page 112 and Appendix E.
[9] Lacouture, *op. cit.*, p. 125.
[10] *ibid.*, p. 125.

customs house in Haiphong. This contravened the terms of the September agreement, and Ho sent a strong protest to Bidault. The French counterclaim suggested that the Vietminh were using Haiphong to import military hardware; and they attempted to prove it by storming a Chinese junk then unloading at the quay. Ho made immediate efforts to quell the resulting clash. Fortunately the local French co-operated and a cease-fire was agreed on. But this by no means pleased the French high command in Saigon, who promptly ordered the French commander in Haiphong to occupy the city in order to teach the Vietminh a lesson. The French commander discovered that he could not successfully re-occupy the city without the help of the French navy. He thereupon called for support from the naval vessel lying at anchor in the harbour, which happened to be the very *Suffren* that two months earlier had been the *agapemone* of Franco-Vietnamese embraces. The *Suffren* shelled the city, slaughtering 6,000 harmless Vietnamese civilians.[11]

Ho did not entirely give up hope. Sainteny was being sent from Paris to sort things out: there might be one last chance. Meanwhile the first president of d'Argenlieu's Cochin-China 'Republic', Nguyen Van Trinh, finding that at best he was a government of one, and at worst a French puppet, hanged himself. D'Argenlieu replaced him with Le Van Hoach, a puppet made of sterner stuff.[12]

Sainteny left Paris on 23 November; but when he reached Saigon, d'Argenlieu, not at all anxious for the North to be interferred with by meddling diplomats, managed to detain him for a week. When at last Sainteny arrived at Hanoi he found Ho in bed seriously ill: stricken down, it was said, by his last ditch fight to prevent the now inevitable holocaust. But a *deus ex machina* again appeared from the wings: on 12 December the vacillating Bidault was replaced by Léon Blum, Ho's socialist friend of the 'twenties. Blum quickly arranged for Moutet to join Sainteny in a joint effort to restore peace. Not waiting for his arrival, Ho sent Blum an urgent letter, requesting that both sides should consider themselves as returning to the *status quo ante*; that is, prior to the first Haiphong incident on 20 November. Since the only communication facilities at that time were via Saigon this letter had to pass through d'Argenlieu's hands: he was able to arrange ten days' delay in transmission.[13] During this time the incidents between French and Vietminh troops steadily mounted. Giap was agitating for an immediate coup inside Hanoi in order to get control of the city. On 19 December Ho sent Sainteny a final message:

The atmosphere is becoming more and more strained at present. That is very regrettable. Pending the decision from Paris I am counting on you to work out with M. Giam[14] some way of improving the climate. Please accept my kindest regards and convey my respects to Madame Sainteny.[15]

[11] See Paul Mus, *Vietnam, Sociologie d'une Guerre*, Lacouture, *op. cit.*, Shaplen, *op. cit.*, and others.
[12] Ellen J. Hammer in *Vietnam, History, Documents and Opinions*, p. 75.
[13] Philippe Devillers, *op. cit.*, p. 352.
[14] Hoang Minh Giam, then Ho's Minister for Foreign Affairs.
[15] Quoted by Lacouture, *op. cit.*, p. 136.

In view of what was to happen that same evening, this letter seems almost unruffled. We can only suppose that Ho himself was unaware of the disaster then about to break: when, only a few hours after receiving this letter, Sainteny was leaving his office, an explosion at the generating plant plunged the city into darkness and at once the shooting started. Sainteny jumped into an armoured vehicle, intending to seek shelter in the citadel. But he had no sooner driven off than the car hit a mine and burst into flames. Managing to extricate himself, Sainteny was luckily picked up by a passing French patrol. It was subsequently discovered he had twenty shrapnel wounds.[16]

The following day, Ho himself had a narrow escape when he and Giap were surrounded by French troops ringing the Presidency. At all costs they could not let themselves be caught. Making a dash for it and heading for the paddy-fields, they escaped under a hail of bullets. It was then late evening. Already the next morning Ho was writing his famous proclamation of 21 December. Addressed to the Vietnamese, to the French and to 'peoples of the Allied Powers', it stated the events (as Ho saw them) of the past two months, blaming the French colonials, not Metropolitan France, for repudiating the agreements made.[17] It appealed to French soldiers not to allow themselves to be dragged into an ignoble war. It appealed to Allied peoples to strive towards a peaceful solution. But above all it appealed to the Vietnamese to be ready to fight. It was not exactly a call to arms: the war had not officially begun. Ho told his army to attack when attacked. Everyone must be ready to defend his country. Those who helped the enemy must be dealt with. But rights of foreigners must be respected and prisoners of war properly treated. 'Our resistance war will be long and painful,' Ho warned, 'but whatever the sacrifices, however long the struggle, we shall fight to the end, until Vietnam is fully independent and reunified.' *Determination, determination. With that one can do everything successfully.*[18] But Ho could scarcely know how far off victory was.

The war began with a few French successes. They had better weapons, both in small arms and artillery. The Vietminh army, despite all Giap's endeavours, were still fighting with a paucity of armaments, mostly obsolete, they had either captured from the Japs or bought piecemeal at fantastic cost from the Chinese troops. In addition to having control of the air the French also had vehicle mobility. The Vietminh had neither planes nor transport.

Leaving Giap to operate tactically, Ho directed overall operations from a hut in the scrub jungle at Tuyen Quang some 60 miles northwest from Hanoi. One might suppose that since his policy of trying to come to terms had failed, Ho's leadership would now be shaken. Yet he continued to direct his country's affairs with even greater prestige. Just as at a time of national peril Britain responded to Churchill and America to Roosevelt, so now Vietnam responded to Ho. But Ho was perhaps an even greater hero to his countrymen because he was never a patrician. He was always able to make the people feel he was one of

---

16 *Histoire d'une Paix Manquée*, quoted by Lacouture, *op. cit.*, p. 137.
17 Thus confirming Pham Van Dong's fears revealed to me in Paris.
18 Quoted by Vo Nguyen Giap as Ho's 'most valuable lesson'. (*Days with Ho Chi Minh*, p. 216).

them: a relationship that both Churchill and Roosevelt were deprived of by their inevitable classification as 'ruling class'.

While conducting his guerrilla war, Ho also sent out, via radio, a continuing stream of peace proposals. But during all this period the stars were continually unfavourable. Blum had now been replaced by Ramadier, who had none of his predecessor's liberal leanings and discounted the peace overtures coming from Vietminh headquarters. Meanwhile, Moutet, whom Blum had despatched to support Sainteny, was likewise held up in Saigon by d'Argenlieu despite all Leclerc's frantic efforts to get him and Ho together. Moutet seems in the end to have been alienated from his former friend and the meeting was never arranged. On 24 January 1947 Ho made another attempt at reconciliation with France by writing to Sainteny. Despite what had happened, they were still friends.

> And I can assure you that our two peoples are still friends, too. There are already enough dead and enough ruins! What are we to do now, you and I? France has only to recognize the independence and unity of Vietnam, and at once hostilities will cease. I am ready to work for peace, a just and honourable peace for our two countries. I hope that you, on your side, will be working to the same end.[19]

But Sainteny had hardly yet recovered from his wounds. Perhaps this is why Ho's letter went unanswered.

In February d'Argenlieu was unexpectedly replaced as High Commissioner by Bollaert; this offered a glimmer of hope. Ho at once sent Bollaert a cease-fire proposal. But de Gaulle intervened personally by warning his new High Commissioner not to cede an inch of 'French territory'. Then Ramadier, as if to close all loopholes against any possible 'peace collaboration', dismissed all his communist ministers, thus ensuring that Ho had no friends on the home front. But the final door still had to be slammed and effectively barred. Paul Mus, scholar, liberal and Far East expert, was either persuaded or manoeuvred into personally taking to Ho, not terms for a cease fire, but a virtual demand for capitulation. On being presented with this cavalier document Ho kept his temper, and he and Mus parted friends; but it was felt nappropriate to drink the bottle of champagne that Ho (almost pathetically, one feels) had put on ice to celebrate a *rapprochement*.[20] The one useful thing that the French might have got out of this visit was ignored: Mus reported back that Ho was still firmly in the saddle and was confident he would win. But Paris preferred to keep its head in the sand.

Already in December Bao Dai had been invited back to France from his refuge in Hong Kong. While naturally reluctant to leave this 'other Eden, demi-paradise', with its charming sing-song girls happily wedded to all mod-cons, Bao Dai nevertheless had a sense of duty. When I happened to meet him there in the Repulse Bay hotel I was surprised to find that not only had Bao Dai kept himself posted about

---

[19] Quoted by Lacouture, *op. cit.*, p. 144.
[20] Paul Mus, *Vietnam, Sociologie d'une Guerre*, quoted by Lacouture, *op. cit.* p. 146.

recent developments but was in fact anxious to make himself useful. One could only feel sorry for this *demodé* prince for whom the word 'useful' could only mean 'being used'.

Bao Dai never pretended that as things stood then he could hope to compete with Ho, either amongst rival parties or in terms of popularity. Having arrived in France, he tried to persuade the government that any arrangement under his leadership must include not only independence but the inclusion of Cochin China with the rest of Vietnam. Anything less, said Bao Dai, would make it impossible for him to form a government. The French reluctantly agreed to his terms, thus conceding the principle of unity they had so stubbornly denied to Ho. But the nature of the 'independence' was nebulous. Even the 'unity' issue could not be fully resolved without first altering a clause in the French constitution.

It required the victory of the communists in China to bring France to the final point of action. Thus, it was not until May 1949 that Cochin China was 'attached to the associated State of Vietnam'. Returning to his country for the first time in three years, Bao Dai was proclaimed 'head of State', a term that would henceforth be increasingly applied to an area that was all head and no state.

Meanwhile, the initial French successes had given way to increasing reverses. They held the towns but lost all the countryside. Then the victory of the communists in China brought Ho a valuable ally. Not only did this neighbour offer military aid, they also recognized Ho's government. The USSR, having so far offered nothing but sympathy, suddenly realized they had been preceded in an important diplomatic move, and were quick to accord their own recognition.[21] When the satellites followed suit Ho found himself transformed from a mere rebel with scarcely a friend to a President with 800 million friends. The American Secretary of State, Dean Acheson, coldly observed that 'this should remove any illusions as to the "nationalist" character of Ho Chi Minh's aims and reveals Ho in his true colours as the mortal enemy of native independence in Indo-China'.[22] The French immediately saw that by turning the war into an anti-communist crusade they could now expect to get American aid.

They got the aid, more and more of it; but they still got no victories. Something else was necessary: a certain support from the Vietnamese people that would offset Ho's hold on the population. Thus the war recently promoted as part of the struggle against international communism quickly had to be presented as a nationalist civil war, with Ho fighting against the 'legitimate' government under Bao Dai.

By this time, France had increased her original 20,000 troops (agreed by the terms of the September 1946 treaty) to 150,000 (about a third of her entire army), which included not only French and Vietnamese, but Moroccans, Senegalese and even a wedge of ex-Nazis who had joined the French Foreign Legion. Despite these forces, the French could control only the major cities and the main lines of communication. On the roads Frenchmen could travel only in convoys and even then could not be sure of reaching their destination. Even in the cities no Frenchman or pro-French Vietnamese was safe at night. Saigon itself was

[21] See McLane, *op. cit.*, pp. 435f.
[22] Dept. of State Bulletin, 13 February 1950, p. 244.

honeycombed with Vietminh units, who even collected taxes from the Chinese and Vietnamese inhabitants. Although the French were spending half their military budget in Indo-China, the greater part of the country was in the hands of their opponents.[23]

During all this period Ho continued, under the stress of war and despite the most severe privations, to write directions to his people. If we cannot compare his literary output, especially in terms of volume, with that of Mao, we need to remember that the Chinese leader not only had long spells of quiet in Yenan, but also after 1953 was comparatively free from external pressures. But in Ho's career there was never a period when he could consider himself free from pressure either internal or external. His selected works add up to four volumes – small enough when compared to Mao's thirty or forty, or even to Lenin's twelve or fourteen.

Ho's directives to the peasants, the soldiers, the political groups and to the people in general, were unremitting. He never ceased to stimulate everybody to greater effort, to hope, to victory. Consider as an example his appeal of 11 June 1948:[24]

Patriotic zeal has a triple end: 1. To conquer famine. 2. To conquer ignorance. 3. To conquer the enemy. And the way to do it is this: Rely on the people's army plus the people's morale in order to obtain: the welfare of the people.

This is why every citizen, whatever his calling, whether he be intellectual, peasant, worker, businessman or soldier, has a duty to

work fast   work well   work hard.

Every Vietnamese, irrespective of age, sex or status must become a fighter on one of these fronts: military, economic, political or cultural. Each one should make real the password: Resistance of the whole people, *total* resistance.

With patriotic zeal, we shall reconstruct our country even while fighting the resistance war.

As to the results of this dedication, here they are:

Everyone will eat his fill and be adequately clothed.
Everyone will know how to read and write.
All our soldiers will have proper subsistence and enough arms.
The nation will become entirely independent and unified.

In order to achieve these ends I ask everyone to dedicate himself:
The old: to encourage youth to help us vigorously in our work.
The children: to outdo each other both in schoolwork and helping their elders.
Merchants and manufacturers: to increase their businesses.
Peasants and workers: to increase their output.
Intellectuals: to create.
Technicians: to invent.
Officials: to serve the people more devotedly.

[23] Ellen Hammer in *Vietnam, History, Documents and Opinions*, p. 81.
[24] *Ho Chi Minh, Écrits*, Foreign Languages Press, Hanoi, 1971, pp. 85/7. (Author's translation.)

Regular army and guerrilla units: to strike even heavier blows against the enemy and particularly to seize weapons.

Do these words mean anything or are they mere platitudes? If we read Churchill's speeches today (or Roosevelt's) they too seem platitudinous. With patriotic speeches it is not alone the words that count but the words coming from that speaker at that time. To delight his audience Churchill had only to say, in his unique style, 'Nah-zee'; and when Roosevelt said 'My friends' it was worth a million man-hours. These facts can be understood only by those who heard the words at the time. Ho's words are simple, direct and certainly to the point: but we can believe in their sincerity only if we happen to believe in him.

Other subjects Ho managed to write about from his hut in the jungle concern the prevention of waste, the improvement of guerrilla tactics, how to do away with red tape, and how artists can help to win the war.

A more significant verbal contribution at this time was Ho's political report in February 1951 to the 2nd Congress of the Vietnam Workers' Party (Lao Dong). As already mentioned, the ICP had been disbanded in 1945 and 'Marxist study groups' set up. In Ho's report reference is made to the '1st Congress' having taken place at Macao in 1935, which implies that Ho viewed the ICP and the Workers' Party as identical. In the earlier versions of the report, Ho offered a justification for the suspension of the former[25] but this was excised from later editions. At the conclusion of the 2nd Congress Ho also announced that the Vietminh had been merged with the Lien Viet (Patriotic Front). This latter amalgamation of parties outside the Vietminh had been organized in 1946 to bring in a wider circle of adherents, particularly in Laos and Cambodia. And it would appear that on this present occasion (1951) Ho wanted to emphasize the unity of Vietnam, Laos and Cambodia by dropping the Vietminh in favour of the Lien Viet. In announcing this he tied it in with 'another great political success to mark the opening of the year', namely, the foundation of the Workers' Party, which appears to indicate that he did, after all, consider this as something different from the ICP.

Ho's report of the Congress[26] summarized the history of the revolutionary movement, recorded the events of the war against the French, outlined the gains made and the faults committed, and warned of the impending contest with the Americans. The report includes, almost for the first time since independence was declared, a certain Party Line approach. Remembering those 800 million friends one can scarcely be surprised. Lenin gets his first mention since the 'twenties: in referring to the *modus vivendi* of September 1946, which so many of Ho's friends as well as his critics had looked at askance, Ho quotes Lenin's words: 'If for the good of the revolution we can work usefully with the bandits, then let's do it'. Ho goes on to say: 'To resist the planes and artillery of the enemy we had only bamboo slivers. But our Party is a Marxist-Leninist Party, we don't see only the present, we also see the future and we put our confidence in the morale and strength of the masses.'

This fresh adherence to the Marxist line had already been manifested

---

[25] See Lacouture, *op. cit.*, p. 148.
[26] *Ho Chi Minh, Écrits*, Full text pp. 102 to 130.

in the welcome Ho gave to Léo Figuères, the leader of the Young Communists. Figuères managed to get to Ho's headquarters in March 1950 via the first ambassadorial team coming from China. He was welcomed in Ho's hut with champagne – not that left over from the abortive Paul Mus visit but (according to Ho) part of recent guerrilla booty. In a similar atmosphere of what seemed relaxed confidence the Frenchman was also shown the leader's vegetable plot, and taken through the flower garden to admire the plunge pool Ho had made by damming a bend of the river. Figuères returned to Paris even more convinced than Mus had been that Ho was going to win. But despite the increasing disillusionment in Metropolitan France, the government were disinclined to listen to any reports from a communist.

Meanwhile, two new and opposing factors had been introduced into the Indo-China war by the outbreak of hostilities in Korea (June 1950). The USSR saw in this conflict the transformation of the Cold War into a military showdown between 'the two camps'[27] and became aware that Ho Chi Minh was the staunchest and certainly the most successful champion in their own camp. The US, on the other hand, now felt free to implement a policy that had already been formulated by Dean Acheson:

> The US Government, convinced that neither national independence nor democratic evolution exist in any area dominated by Soviet imperialism, considers the situation to be such as to warrant its according economic aid and military equipment to the associated States of Indo-China and to France in order to assist them in restoring stability and permitting these States to pursue their peaceful and democratic development.[28]

On 27 June this policy was endorsed more specifically by President Truman, who announced 'acceleration in the furnishing of military assistance to the forces of France and the associated states in Indo-China and the despatch of a military mission to provide close working relations with these forces.'[29]

But while there was to be increasing evidence of US help to France and South Vietnam, the only immediate result of the new Soviet concern for the North was shown in the attitude of the French Communist Party, with Thorez taking up the rallying cry already put out by Figuères in favour of a new campaign against 'the dirty war'. This gave the French and American governments further excuses to call Ho a tool of the Comintern. Nevertheless, more and more Frenchmen agreed with Thorez about the real nature of the war, so that new troops sent out to reinforce the weary veterans in Indo-China brought with them,

[27] The phrase employed by Zhdanov when in September 1947 the Cominform was founded and the USSR promoted a new militant policy *vis-à-vis* the West.

[28] Statement made 8 May 1950 and reported in Department of State Bulletin, 22 May 1950, p. 821.

[29] Department of State Bulletin, 5 July 1950, p. 5. The military mission arrived in Saigon ten days afterwards. See also William Warbey, *Vietnam: the truth*. The Merlin Press, 1965, p. 37.

not a morale boost but a miasma of pessimism. The French government began to discover what the US government had to learn later at the same tragic cost: that for a democracy to fight a war without full support at home is ultimately impossible. The French army vainly held control of the air, the sea, the towns and all main roads. Although the Vietminh held nothing materially except the countryside, they also had the greatest weapon of all time (with the possible exception of the H-bomb): a leader with the fixed belief that he would win. This confidence (plus no doubt the addition of some useful Chinese equipment) enabled Ho in late 1950 to stage a victorious offensive in northern Tonkin. And when, early the following year, the French released official figures of the cost of the war it was revealed that they had already suffered some nineteen thousand casualties at a cost equivalent to two billion US dollars.[30]

Nevertheless, during the period of the Korean war (June 1950 to June 1953), the war in Indo-China became of secondary global interest. While the two sides slogged it out, Ho, Nehru, certain French liberals, and various goodwill organizations like the Congress for the Independence of the Colonial Peoples sponsored by Fenner Brockway in England, tried to get mediation started.[31] Unfortunately Bidault, who had then become Minister of Foreign Affairs, showed his former intransigence in listening to these overtures. It was purely extraneous circumstances that finally forced his hand. In March 1953 the death of Stalin would have led to an immediate détente between the two great political camps (and thus to an attempt to end the Vietnam war) had it not been for the continuing Korean war. The cessation of this in June opened the path towards a general easing of tension, but again it was chance that led to a possible way out: in October a Swedish journalist, Sven Löfgren, effected an exchange of communications with Ho which revealed the leader's desire for a 'negotiated armistice' if the French would respond.[32] But Bidault, in the face of growing domestic murmurs, snubbed this overture; and it was not until the following February that a conference was called at Berlin to tackle (amongst other problems) the Vietnam war. For a further three months Bidault, encouraged by the US, managed to stave off that evil day when (as he put it) 'France would, by responding to Ho's peace overtures, restore Vietminh confidence and give it sustenance.' Thus it was not until 8 May 1954 that the Indo-China phase of the Geneva Conference opened 'under singularly unpropitious circumstances, the garrison at Dien Bien Phu having succumbed on the previous day'.[33] 'Unpropitious' is perhaps a euphemism: with the capitulation at Dien Bien Phu, French power in Indo-China had collapsed.

[30] *The New York Times*, 4 January 1951.
[31] Lacouture, *op. cit.*, p. 150.
[32] McLane, *op. cit.*, p. 463.
[33] *Vietnam, History, Documents and Opinions*, p. 131.

11 Prometheus

Without the cold and desolation of winter
There could not be the warmth and splendour of spring.
Calamity has tempered and hardened me,
And turned my mind into steel.

In March 1954 John Foster Dulles, then Secretary of State, had made a speech not only openly associating America with the French cause in Indo-China but threatening united action 'if the aggressor got any more Chinese help'.[1] Meanwhile, Nehru had initiated a Peace Conference aimed at settling not only the Indo-China war but various lesser Asian problems, such as the unsatisfactory aftermath of the Korean war.[2] The US was against such a conference for two reasons: first, Nehru was on their black-list for having opposed the Korean war; and second, they considered any suggestion of 'peace' to be pro-communist.[3] They reluctantly agreed, however, to talk about the issue of Berlin, then about a final settlement on Korea, and finally to 'informal discussions' about Vietnam. In regard to this third item, Richard Nixon (then Vice-President) gave a prior statement of the American stand, along the lines of Dulles's 'domino theory': that if South Vietnam were taken by the Communists, other Asiatic countries would fall to the Communists one by one like a row of stacked dominoes; and the United States did not intend to let that happen. 'Unfortunately' Nixon continued, 'French pressure will be exerted at the conference for negotiation and the end of the fighting. The British will take a similar position, because of mounting Labour Party pressure and defections in the Conservative ranks. . . . This country is the only nation strong enough at home to take a position that will save Asia.'[4]

In order that America might achieve this rescue operation, Dulles, acting for President Eisenhower, called a meeting of the various US department heads and proposed that several hundred planes – some on carriers in the South China Sea and some based in the Philippines – should go to the aid of the French then encircled at Dien Bien Phu. After lengthy discussions it was decided that although America was powerful enough to do this alone, her position would be weakened on the diplomatic front unless she could bring in on the deal at least the British. Thus, on the very eve of a conference that had been called to pursue a peace settlement, Dulles asked Eden (then Foreign Secretary) to agree that the use of US planes should be presented as 'united action'. Eden demurred, on the grounds that the use of planes would, as always, call for follow-up troops, with the United Kingdom being asked to

---

[1] *Vietnam, History, Documents and Opinions*, p. 97.
[2] Warbey, *op. cit.*, pp. 39 and 41.
[3] This is to simplify two very complicated issues; my purpose here is only to indicate the strained atmosphere of the subsequent Geneva Conference.
[4] Quoted in the *New York Times*, 17 April 1954.

contribute. Some of this discussion leaked. To still the spate of rumours Churchill felt compelled to announce in the House of Commons that the United Kingdom had *not* entered into any military commitments; at which there was a burst of cheering. Eden went off to Geneva feeling he now had a mandate to negotiate peace. For the Americans, on the other hand, the Conference opened in an atmosphere of gloom, to be at once made Stygian by the news of the French defeat at Dien Bien Phu.[5]

Historically this battle might take its place alongside Creasey's *Fifteen Decisive Battles of the World*. It was the first time in three centuries of colonialism that Asian troops defeated a Western conqueror in open battle. This had come about largely because the French commander, General Henri Navarre, seeing nothing ahead but years of guerrilla warfare that would take France to the conference table without a card in her hand, devised the so called Navarre Plan whereby the French armies would concentrate their strength in key positions. One of the points chosen was Dien Bien Phu, which controlled the Vietminh link-up with their allies in Laos (the Pathet Lao) as well as the supply routes coming in from China.

In choosing Dien Bien Phu for his most significant build-up Navarre overlooked two vital considerations. First, that unlike conditions in Europe where supply routes need roads, here in Vietnam the Vietminh could man-handle their supplies through circuitous routes; second, that the French themselves did depend on roads, failing which everything had to be brought in by air; they were separated from their base at Hanoi by 300 miles of roads that were constantly vulnerable to enemy attack as well as to adverse weather.

Thus, instead of hunting down and annihilating the enemy, the French found themselves suddenly ringed by Vietminh troops who had unbelievably man- and pony-hauled, through 'impassable' jungles, 200 heavy guns as well as multi-tube rocket launchers; and this concentration of artillery was slowly reducing the exposed French gun sites to heaps of rubble.

To try and save the situation the French command parachuted in additional guns and troops. This took up the vital air transport space that should have been given over to supplying the existing garrison.

When the siege began, it had about eight days' worth of supplies on hand and required 200 tons a day to maintain minimum levels. The sheer magnitude of preparing that mass of supplies for parachuting was solved only by superhuman feats of the airborne supply units on the outside – efforts more than matched by the heroism of the soldiers inside the valley, who had to crawl into the open, under fire, to collect the cannisters.[6]

How did the Vietminh manage to supply their own forces? Thousands of men, women and even children forming the supply units walked along the jungle tracks at night with their loads on poles, minute oil lamps furnishing the pin points of light that enabled them to follow

[5] See *Vietnam, History, Documents and Opinions*, pp. 125f.
[6] *Vietnam, History, Documents and Opinions*, p. 120.

each other in unending human chains. Rice constituted the bulk of the supplies. Only one-tenth of each man's burden could hope to reach its destination: the remaining nine-tenths went to feed the carriers on their long march.[7]

Rightly enough, Giap is given credit for this victory. Nevertheless, it is Ho's name that will go down in history as the essential victor. In a war for independence of remarkable similarity (and with a similar capitulation), the battle of Saratoga was won by Horatio Gates, a general of considerable reputation at the time. But today, few of us will have heard of Gates; and Washington rightly gets the glory. *Dux erat ille ducum*[8] must apply to all great leaders.

Giap having won the military victory, it was Pham Van Dong's turn to try for equal success at the conference table. We may be sure that just as Ho stood behind Giap on the battlefield, so he now stood behind Dong at the conference table. What direction to take at this vital moment in Vietnam history must have been Ho's biggest challenge yet. On the face of it, he had won a smashing victory at the exact moment when a conference was already scheduled to seek the path of peace. It seemed as if he had only to state his terms; if not accepted he could then continue the war and drive out what was left of the French army. But Ho knew, the French knew, everyone knew, that the Americans were poised to strike. Because of recalcitrant allies they had not been quite ready to save Dien Bien Phu; but if the war were now renewed, they were ready to go it alone. Moreover, there was more than a possibility they would use The Bomb. At this period, the reality of the H-bomb had not yet convinced the Powers that nuclear warfare spelled total disaster to winner and loser alike. America was then still thinking in terms of Hiroshima: a single sharp lesson, no doubt slightly more destructive, would be all that would be necessary to force Ho to his knees. Meanwhile, the Russians knew that, atom bomb or no atom bomb, the American entry into North Vietnam would bring in the Chinese to protect their border, just as had happened in Korea. Furthermore, Russia felt that this time she could hardly afford to be left out of a conflict that might eliminate China and leave the one big enemy supremely powerful. At all costs, confrontation must be avoided; Ho must come to terms. It was therefore with a Russian ultimatum that Pham Van Dong had to acquaint his chief. Thus, despite the fact that Ho held all the aces, the Americans were able to produce, from up their sleeve, a decisive trump.

Dulles, in fact, presented himself at the conference with the air of a headmaster addressing truant pupils: 'We hope to find that the aggressors come here in a mood to purge themselves of their aggression', he told the Press.[9] Never before in history, surely, did a victor find himself more circumscribed by friend and foe alike. Ho at this time was holding four-fifths of all Vietnam, North and South. The 'government' in the South (Bao Dai and his henchmen) had almost no following amongst the people: what little jurisdiction it did have was dependent on the remaining French army – already crippled, and soon to be withdrawn.

[7] See *From Colonialism to Communism*, p. 67.
[8] He was a leader of leaders: Ovid.
[9] Quoted in the *New York Times*, 25 April 1954.

Despite all this, Dong had to sign away half the whole territory: this was the price the Americans demanded, and which the Russians and the Chinese (neither of them wanting the alternative confrontation) made Ho pay. The one concession was the promise of elections in the South 'within two years'. Meanwhile Ho was required to withdraw all his troops from that area. The French in turn were to withdraw theirs from the North.

The Americans now produced two additional trump cards. Having supported terms that effectively sealed off Ho in one half of Vietnam, they recognized the southern half as the 'State of Vietnam' while not recognizing his half. This gave a semblance of legality to the South and illegality to the North that was to be constantly stressed in American propaganda during the next decade. The other trump card was simply to withdraw themselves from any official relationship with the Conference and refuse to be associated with the terms of the Agreements. This enabled them to reject any responsibility for implementation.

The protocol of the Geneva Conference was this: the Agreements[10] were between France and the Democratic Republic of Vietnam (i.e. Ho's government). The delegates of these two countries, as the belligerent powers, were the *only signatories*. The UK, the USSR, China, Laos and Cambodia, verbally (but officially) approved the terms. Eden representing the UK, Molotov representing the USSR, were co-Chairmen of the Conference, and thus took a special (but undesignated) responsibility for seeing that the terms were met. The US merely 'noted' the terms, making a unilateral, (totally independent) statement as to their own position, which gave them all the desired loopholes. An International Commission, consisting of Canada (anti-Communist), Poland (Communist), and India (neutral) was appointed to police the implementation of the terms. During the subsequent years this commission reported on developments, accusing both North Vietnam and the US of violating the clause about introducing troops, and South Vietnam and the US of preventing elections. The Commission repeatedly appealed to the two co-Chairmen of the Conference that action should be taken. But no action was taken.

Ho was thus forced by overwhelming outside pressures into leaving the vital matter of elections solely in French hands. He had to withdraw from the South *now*, he was committed before the world to do so, and he did indeed do so. Furthermore, the State of Vietnam (that is, South Vietnam under the puppet government) was declared to the world as being a reality *now*, which gave the Americans the opportunity to make it a continuing reality. But in regard to the promised elections (which according to most observers would have given Ho an easy majority),[11] these were to come *later*. And who would see that these elections took place? Before the two years had elapsed, the French withdrew their troops from the South,[12] and left the area under the control of the US-

---

[10] Full terms of these Agreements, together with subsequent Declarations, can be found in *Vietnam, History, Documents and Opinions*, pp. 144–68.

[11] See for example *Vietnam, History, Documents and Opinions*, pp. 167/74.

[12] *ibid.*, p. 169: 'One of the most curious of modern imperialist manoeuvres' comments the editor. It would seem likely that the French were under US pressure. See also *Peace in Vietnam*, p. 41.

sponsored 'State of Vietnam', which naturally did not want elections that would give Ho a victory. They were able to say that as they had never signed the Geneva Agreements it was no responsibility of theirs to see that elections were held. Furthermore, despite Eden's genuine desire to implement the agreed terms, the British Conservative government could ill afford to offend the Americans over something that was not even in their own interest. The United Nations were also valueless to Ho: at this period they were in effect controlled by a majority vote favouring US requirements. As for the Russians and Chinese, they had no way, short of war, to get the elections held. Thus it came about that they never were held, and Ho was effectively deprived of the one benefit the Agreements offered him.

Meanwhile, in July 1954, the US, tired of what they considered Bao Dai's vacillation, had installed a new and more vigorous head of State, Ngo Dinh Diem. His dictatorship under their initial aegis and subsequent disillusion was to last eight years until, to the relief of almost everyone, he was assassinated.[13]

If US behaviour during this period seems something less than equitable we need to remember that her government acted in the pragmatical belief that the end justifies the means: that end being to halt communism. When the communists, whether Russian, Chinese or Vietnamese, fulminated against 'American imperialism' this confirmed their opinion that it was a matter of 'crush or be crushed'. Since the Russian revolution they have pursued a policy of almost unremitting antagonism to communism. Periodic *détentes* (as with China in the spring of 1972) hardly seem to affect their overall conduct.

It was thus inevitable that Ho should find himself between the communist and capitalist millstones. Those in the capitalist camp would say this was his own fault. For example:

A man of Ho's intelligence and political experience could not have but known that to transform a nationalist resistance movement into a militant communist body would be certain to result in the supply of US military aid to France. America would provide such assistance, not to rob the Vietnamese of national independence, for American sentiment was strongly anti-colonialist, but to fight the spread of communism in Asia . . . the decision evinced a callous disregard for the sufferings of his own people.[14]

It was not because of 'sufferings', however, that Ho's countrymen began to grumble, but because Pham Van Dong returned from Geneva with a treaty more suited to defeat than victory. It took all Ho's skill to calm the critics. In particular, Le Duan (himself a southerner, and essentially a militant), complained that Dong (thereby implicating Ho) had conceded too much. Even what was promised, said Le Duan, would prove an ultimate cheat. The French having lost their will to win, the Vietminh should have pursued their fight to total victory. As things were, the promise of elections would not be fulfilled and the Vietminh would have

[13] See p. 121.
[14] P. J. Honey, *op cit.*, p. 41.

to fight to re-capture the entire South instead of the limited territory the French had then been holding.[15]

Le Duan proved right on all these points. Nevertheless Ho was 'more right' in putting the immediate value of the Agreements over their future compliance. Not at that time understanding the art of statecraft as Ho understood it, Le Duan failed to appreciate that an international agreement, no matter how honest or dishonest the participants, is always worth the *immediate and actual* compliance rather than the dubious implementation of promises about the future. (See Appendix E.)

Ho tried to make Le Duan and similar critics understand that although the Vietminh could indeed have totally defeated the French they could not also have totally defeated the Americans.[16] For that task (which Ho already saw as inevitable) intense preparation plus Russian and Chinese support would be necessary.

In France, Mendès-France, a liberal, had succeeded to the Premiership. Anxious to give North Vietnam a square deal, he sent out (November 1954) the one man Ho trusted – Jean Sainteny. But because France had recognized the puppet régime in the South as the official 'State of Vietnam', Mendès-France found himself unable to give Sainteny full diplomatic status as ambassador. Unfortunately, too, the economic and technical expertise that Ho would have gladly sought from France were denied to him because it was felt in French business circles that the marriage between France and North Vietnam was at best only a flirtation. Sainteny tried to build up friendship; but his efforts were negated by three adverse circumstances: France recognized the régime in Saigon; France dared not quarrel with her overwhelming creditor, the United States; above all France was now planning to withdraw her troops from the south, thus forgoing her obligations to implement the elections. Sainteny's goodwill mission was jeopardized at the start, vitiated in the process and totally marred in the conclusion. It was Sainteny himself who wrecked a subsequent visit two years later: when the Hungarian patriots under Imre Nagy rose futilely against their Stalinist government (October 1956), there were eight Hungarian technicians in Hanoi who were openly in sympathy with Nagy. The Hungarian government called for their return; Ho had no recourse but to agree. But these Hungarians prevailed on Sainteny to smuggle them out of the city to asylum in France. This act was humanely admirable but politically invidious: Ho himself was blamed by the Hungarians for an unfriendly act. This strained his relations with Soviet Russia and the Ho-Sainteny friendship was thus killed for ten whole years.

In addition to these problems of foreign relations, Ho was beset with internal stresses. Already in 1953, when more finances were needed for the war, an oppressive campaign was launched to collect more taxes. Over-zealous tax-officials pursued what amounted to terror tactics in their efforts to collect. When Ho learned that many defaulters had been

---

[15] See for example, P. J. Honey, *Genesis of a Tragedy*, Ernest Benn, 1968. Lacouture (*op. cit.*, p. 192) suggests that Ho, in accepting the Russian ultimatum, 'served the immediate interests of world Communism' rather than the preservation of his country.

[16] See for example Lacouture, *op. cit.*, p. 154.

shot he was said to have wept. But certain of his critics, not without justice, hold him personally responsible.[17]

In 1956 an even worse grievance was inflicted on the rural population by the imposition of a land reform campaign along the lines of Mao's own doctrines. This campaign appears to have been instigated partly in the belief that such methods would increase production and partly because at this period Ho was favouring a pro-Chinese policy, having perhaps remembered that it was China who had given the Democratic Republic of Vietnam its first significant recognition, as well as the subsequent help that had led to the victory at Dien Bien Phu. Sino-Vietnamese Friendship Associations were set up throughout North Vietnam, and the land reform campaign was presented as another proof of the close ties existing between China and the DRV.

But attempts at collectivization were bitterly resented by the peasants, whose nature it is always to resist such methods. An uprising in Nghe An, birthplace of the Xo-Viets[18] and Ho's own native province, seemed like an almost personal rebuke against the leader. According to Lacouture[19] 'the repression that followed probably cost tens of thousands of lives'. A sterner critic, Dr Alyn Glyn, makes an even more sweeping indictment: 'About 100,000 farmers and agriculturalists who stood in the way of these Communist agricultural methods were exterminated, and, as an example, in Interzone IV, Ho Chi Minh had to employ an entire division to put down a revolt by the small farmers, 2,000 of whom were killed or removed to other areas.'[20]

The DRV was so shaken by these events that as a scapegoat no less a figure than Truong Chinh, one of the original founders of the Vietminh and then the powerful Party Secretary, was removed from his post, which Ho himself took over.[21] He at once introduced a more rational policy, only to be caught up in the web of another Maoist experiment, 'Let a Hundred Flowers Bloom' (a poetical tag to suggest new freedom of expression for artists and intellectuals). As a result of this new freedom there were, in November 1956, long bouts of self-criticism within the Party, including a *mea culpa* from Giap. But soon afterwards an outburst of critical protest that came to be known as the Intellectuals Revolt was put down with severe reprisals even against such top figures as Tran Duc Thao, whose only crime was that he employed his exceptional mind in philosophic speculation transcending Party dogma. At the same time liberal journals were automatically banned.[22]

---

[17] For example, P. J. Honey, *op. cit.*, p. 15, who adds 'As in most communist states, the vast majority of the people in North Vietnam have not supported the doctrine of communism and still do not approve of it. The communist régime was imposed on North Vietnam by Ho Chi Minh's clever exploitation of Vietnam's nationalism, which was nationwide, for his own communist ends.'

[18] See p. 53.

[19] *op. cit.*, p. 202.

[20] *Witness to Vietnam*, p. 180.

[21] Lacouture, *op. cit.*, says (p. 162) that this was because 'the people were crying out for him', but it seems more likely they were merely crying out.

[22] *ibid.*, pp. 167 and 202.

To understand this apparent injustice under a leader whose life in general reflects a concern both for justice and the arts, we need to remember the structure of the Communist State that then existed in DRV. First, there was a political hierarchy of some eight or ten top men: those leaders of whom Ho was the leader. Following the methods inculcated in the Bac Bo cave, all top policy continued to be discussed democratically and a collective decision taken, even though Ho himself might have the last word. But each decision had, of course, to be translated into action, and it was the method of action that counted. Certainly that group of eight or ten had power of life or death, subject only to the counter-forces that might be exerted from other directions. Of what did these counter-forces consist?

There was first of all the Party, easily the strongest and most effective power group. Then came the army, also very strong, not only because of its numerical strength but because the continuing existence of the state depended on it. Third, there were the peasants, who were not only strong numerically but held their own special key to life or death through food production. Fourth, the labour force: here in Vietnam not as strong as it would be in a more industrialized society, but still fairly powerful. Fifth, the managers and technicians (mostly civil servants), who could not safely be ignored, especially in a country where they were in short supply. Sixth, the educational body, important to the state, but something short of vital as compared with the foregoing. Last and least came the writers, artists and intellectuals, who were to be considered 'useful' only in as far as they could be 'used'. Indeed, they hardly counted as a power group, and they could organize no effective protest. Thus, the 'hundred flowers' could not bloom because, despite the head gardener's general concern, there were too many vigorous trees, bushes and vegetables (not to mention weeds) to crowd them out.

In October of this same year (1957) Ho demonstrated that whatever guidance he might take from Mao he still had close ties with the Soviet Union: we find him attending personally the 40th anniversary celebrations of the Russian revolution held that month in Moscow. Lacouture quotes P. J. Honey in support of a theory that the DRV faction inclining towards the Chinese[23] utilized Ho's absence to promote increased alignment with Peking, and even mentions 'an attempt to seize power'.[24] But in the event it seems to have been Ho's new Soviet orientation that prevailed. This was now the Krushchev era, and Ho succeeded in establishing such good relations with the Soviet leader that for the next five years DRV appears to have leaned towards the USSR rather than towards China. When, at the end of 1958, Mao inaugurated the Great Leap Forward (including promotion of the communes) Ho soon made it clear, by announcing this fact to the world press, that he did not intend to follow the Chinese leader's example.[25]

In February 1960 Ho presented a lengthy economic and social report to commemorate the 30th anniversary of the founding of 'the Party', with a specific reference to the fact that in 1951 it had changed its name

[23] See page 120 herein.
[24] *ibid.*, p. 203.
[25] *Washington Post*, 20 January 1959.

from the ICP to the Workers' Party. Ho covers the general march of events up to 1957, including the emergence of the Vietminh, the subsequent war against the French, the Geneva agreements, and the resulting American encroachments. He then more specifically deals with developments in the matter of land reform, industrial progress, and social improvement. The claims in connection with the first ignore the price paid in human suffering. As for relations with the USSR and China, the names of both powers are coupled in a joint tribute. We may note, however, that throughout the report emphasis is laid upon Marxism-Leninism as the foundation upon which the edifice of DRV had been built. And two months later we find Ho writing the much-quoted article entitled 'The Path to Leninism', in which he gives an unreserved tribute to the significance of the Russian leader without a mention of Mao.

Honey also says[26] that Ho again went to Moscow in August 1960 'to conclude an agreement with Krushchev' at a time of 'bad relations' between the Soviet Union and China, and that Krushchev promised industrial help. But it seems that Ho then took care to pay his respects to Mao by visiting Peking on his way home.

Meanwhile, in April 1956, France had withdrawn her forces from South Vietnam. This was some three months before the final date (20 July) for the proposed elections and re-unification. Although the French troops were probably too few to have forced Diem to accept the elections, the mere fact of French departure gave him a free hand to ignore any further pressure or suggestions in this regard, no matter from what source. Ho had to inform his people that since the elections would not now be held only a long hard struggle could hope to re-unify the country. Pham Van Dong had been sent to Delhi to secure Nehru's support in getting the International Control Commission (of which India was a member) to enforce the agreements. Unfortunately for North Vietnam, the Commission could only report, it could not take action. Only strenuous Soviet pressure could effect any real change. This was no doubt largely in Ho's mind when he himself had gone to Moscow at the end of 1957. But during all this period, the USSR was occupied with other problems, including Nasser, Hungary and Krushchev's efforts to promote the prevailing Soviet policy of 'peaceful co-existence'. Having already sent a continual flow of exhortations to Saigon, 'all rejected out of hand',[27] Ho made proposals in the spring of 1958 to re-establish at least free movement on the frontier between the two zones, to permit the exchange of goods and more especially the importation of rice into the North, which had always been dependent on the South for this vital commodity. It had never been intended at the Geneva Conference that the 'temporary' splitting of the country at the 17th parallel should become an economic split. But Diem had then made it so, and nothing was permitted to cross. No Berlin wall was ever as impregnable as that 17th parallel spun from diplomatic gossamer. Thus, in addition to all other circumventions, the Geneva agreements were also used as a way to starve the North.

However, if during these difficult years there was something less than

26 *op. cit.*, p. 77.
27 Lacouture, *op. cit.*, p. 223.

full accord and happiness in North Vietnam, in the South there was general misery. As we have seen, the Americans replaced Bao Dai with Ngo Dinh Diem, an American-educated Catholic. Since less than a tenth of the people were Catholics his Catholicism had no general appeal; but it did have the effect of pulling from the North several more hundred thousand Catholics, as well as a few hundred thousand non-Catholics who for one reason or other found Ho's régime irksome. This vast increase in population, most of whom flocked into the towns, caused widespread inflation and food shortages. The general disorder from the recent war was aggravated by the growing indifference of the French administrators and business people who were now pulling out. To get things in order Ngo Dinh Diem was given full backing by the Americans. He was even given more. Despite their manipulation of the Geneva Conference, American plans had been set back by the French defeat and they had instigated an anti-Communist front called the South East Asia Treaty Organization (SEATO) consisting of Britain, France, Australia, New Zealand, Pakistan, Philippines, Thailand, and themselves, dedicated to stopping any further communist 'aggression' in the States of Cambodia, Laos and Vietnam. Thus Diem was given a wholesale guarantee of protection not only by America but by all these states collectively. No reservations were put upon the type of government he might introduce; and in the case of internal opposition he had only to cry communist to get full backing for any reprisals he chose to inflict. He had no intention, of course, of permitting the promised elections and with American support was able to stifle every effort Ho made towards getting them implemented.[28]

As we have seen, under the terms of the Geneva Agreements Ho had been required to withdraw all Vietminh troops from the South. But even after this was completed there were hundreds of thousands of pro-Vietminh guerrillas who had gone back to their farms but were still on the alert. Diem's policy of terror was therefore soon returned with terror. But whereas his own acts of violence were indiscriminately aimed at all those amongst the populace he considered hostile, the Vietminh[29] selected their targets only amongst Diem's own agents, whose violent death troubled almost no one. Thus, while Diem alienated the peasant population, the Vietminh won support from almost everybody except the Catholics.[30] What began as a series of terroristic acts followed by reprisals and counter-reprisals soon expanded into the steady conflict of a full-scale war.

For at least four years, Ho endeavoured as far as he was able to stay out of this particular conflict, knowing that the Americans anticipated his more active resistance and needed only this excuse to launch a full-scale war. He therefore limited himself to protocol, hammering home the terms of the Geneva treaty, appealing to France and to the co-Chairmen of the Conference, Eden and Molotov. But France and

---

[28] Towards the end of his dictatorship he was able to rig any election to give himself a thumping majority.

[29] Here in the south more often called the Vietcong, a name originally coined by Diem as a contemptuous term and later taken up by the Americans. They were soon to form themselves into the National Liberation Front (NLF)

[30] See *Vietnam, History, Documents and Opinions*, pp. 234f.

Britain, as well as being concerned with the Geneva treaty, were signatories to SEATO and therefore turned deaf ears (and sometimes scarlet cheeks) to all Ho's appeals.

By 1960 internal pressures at last forced Ho to take action against Diem's all-out campaign of suppression, which was inevitably killing off the best men in the southern resistance movement. In the previous year Diem had introduced 'Law 10/59' which inflicted the death penalty on almost anybody without trial.[31] A policy of open terror as part of the law of the country was in line with Hitler at his worst.

It was at this time that Le Duan was made Secretary of the Party (a post which since Truong Chinh's demotion had been filled by Ho himself). This key position going to a southern militant altered the direction of the Vietminh policy; the activities of the southern resistance movement now became the prime concern of the Hanoi régime. Towards the end of the year the units of what Diem called the Vietcong formed themselves into the organization destined to become almost as famous as the Vietminh itself: the National Liberation Front (NLF). The United States propaganda machine depicted this as merely the tool of Hanoi. In asserting that the NLF was all front and no national liberation the Americans chose to ignore the reality: that most of the population in the South backed this organization because it was their own. One reason for the later American atrocities (a terrifying urge to kill everything that moved) was that the American troops could not understand why everybody was against them in a country where they were supposed to be the liberators; fighting, so they had been told, on behalf of a *majority* who were terrified by communist infiltrators and only longing to be saved. The realization that almost every man's hand was against them came as a demoralizing shock. An American writing about the Vietnam war puts the case succinctly: 'The United States have three enemies. One is the Vietcong, one is the South Vietnamese; but their biggest enemy is themselves – their dedication to a lie, a swindle. A deceived nation cannot win wars.'[32]

The appointment of Le Duan as Party Secretary was also significant as part of the new pro-Soviet orientation. Not the least impressive aspect of Ho's overall strategy was his diplomatic skill in steering a course amidst the rocks first of internecine Soviet strife, then of the even more dangerous Sino-Soviet relations. 'It was a remarkable tribute to the sagacity of Ho that he was always able to steer a safe path between China and Soviet Union'.[33] The purges, the death of

[31] For text, see *Vietnam, History, Documents and Opinions*, p. 268.

[32] William J. Lederer, *The Anguished American*, Gollancz, 1969. In naming the South Vietnamese as the third enemy, the author produces pages of facts and statistics, drawn up from his own observations and those of many other correspondents of varying nationalities, showing how large elements of the population devoted themselves to exploiting the war: plundering American *matériel*, speculating in currency, selling drugs, organizing vice dens, hoarding and cornering commodities, selling stolen American arms to the Vietcong, and outrageously profiteering in every form of enterprise associated with the war effort. According to Lederer this corruption permeates every class of society from top to bottom.

[33] P. J. Honey, *op. cit.*, p. 77.

Stalin, the rise and fall of Krushchev:[34] none of these seemed to shake Ho. And when we remember that he additionally kept both Chinese and Soviet friendship despite their ensuing enmity we begin to feel that Old Man Ho might be called the master diplomat of all time.[35]

The very composition of his cabinet reflects his skill in walking this Chinese-Soviet tightrope. Against the Soviet-leaning Giap we have the pro-Chinese Truong Chinh – both men of the top calibre. Supporting Truong Chinh is the almost equally powerful Nguyen Duy Trinh as Minister of Foreign Affairs. Supporting Giap (although he often takes a mediating position) is Ho's right-hand man, Pham Van Dong. Another influential figure, Le Duc Tho (largely a theoretician) inclines towards the Chinese. In 1960 it was considered useful, not to say necessary, to bring into the hierarchy another pro-Soviet member: Le Duan served admirably.

The next step was to convene the 3rd Party Congress (September 1960). It is an indication of Ho's solidarity with international communism that despite stresses and the barriers of distance he was able to welcome comrades not only from the USSR and satellite countries but also from China, North Korea, France, India, Indonesia, Japan, Canada and Mongolia. Re-affirming his complete allegiance to world communism, Ho promised 'to pursue the struggle against Diem and his American masters'. It was in this somewhat oblique fashion that Ho for the first time publicly announced that the war with the US had begun.

[34] In 1960 came the Summit Conference and the break with the US that led to the Cuban crisis. This for Krushchev was the beginning of his end.
[35] But Ho did of course always hold the master trump. It was the Vietnamese themselves who fought the US to a standstill. Not one soldier did the USSR or China contribute to the abrasion of their 'enemy'.

12 Victor

How much the rice must suffer under the pestle!
But after the pounding it comes out white like cotton.
The same thing often happens to men in this world:
Misfortune's workshop turns them to polished jade.

United States intervention in Vietnam had begun as far back as 1950, when Acheson promised 'military and economic aid to France and the associated states'. With the outbreak of the Korean war the following year, this promise was rapidly made into an effective reality. At the time of Dien Bien Phu, the US was indeed on the brink of full-scale war.

Most of the aid had gone to France; but after the Geneva settlement everything went to the régime of Ngo Dinh Diem and his successors. This aid was stepped up year by year; in 1960, the International Control Commission itself 'sorrowfully noted large imports of US arms and material into Vietnam'.[1] It was largely in response to this increasing aid (but also to Diem's terror tactics) that Ho appointed a southerner, Le Duan, in the position of Party Secretary, and subsequently elected to support the newly-formed National Liberation Front.

In December 1961 President Kennedy wrote personally to Diem with promises of increased help, which was, indeed, at once forthcoming. Within a few months the ICC was again censuring the US for continued and increasing violations of the Geneva Agreements.[2]

In November 1963 Diem was murdered by some of his rivals who had found there was no other way to get a voice in government.[3] Diem had long since proved a dangerously-independent autocrat, and Kennedy could only breathe a sigh of relief that he was now conveniently disposed of, so that the US could proceed without interference towards its real objective: the elimination of the NLF. With the accomplishment of that task, an effective anti-communist bastion could be established in South Vietnam along the lines of that recently imposed on South Korea. But within a few weeks Kennedy himself was assassinated. In the resulting atmosphere of alarm and hysteria, Johnson,

[1] *Vietnam, History, Documents and Opinions*, p. 463.
[2] *ibid.* But they were now also censuring the DRV for aiding the NLF.
[3] A full history of the life and death of Ngo Dinh Diem is given in *Vietnam, History, Documents and Opinions*, pp. 201 to 295 – which contains articles by various writers. Confirming the general obloquy the Editor, Professor Marvin E. Gettleman, adds this comment: 'A huge literature documenting these phenomena is readily available. See John Mecklin, *Mission in Torment: An Intimate Account of the U.S. Role in Vietnam* (Garden City, N.Y., 1965), chapter III; Malcolm W. Browne, *The New Face of War* (Indianapolis/Kansas City/New York, 1965), especially chapter IX; David Halberstam, *The Making of Quagmire* (New York, 1964).'

rather more anti-communist than his predecessor,[4] was easily persuaded
by the Pentagon to step up the war programme.

For the United States, however, the immediate problem was not so
much to give aid to South Vietnam as to find a régime such aid might
safely be given to. Getting rid of Diem had been difficult; but replacing
him proved even more difficult. We have only to examine the list of
'heads of State' to see the grand guignol that constituted South Vietnamese politics during these next few years.

After a mere two months, the first military régime was overthrown by
General Nguyen Kanh. Seven months later the general was in turn
ousted by Dr Nguyen Xuan Oanh. But the general shortly staged a
counter-coup and re-instated himself. His second reign was even shorter
than the first: a month at most. Saigon's mayor, Tran Van Huong, who
replaced him, lasted three months. He in turn was ousted by the re-
emergence of Dr Oanh, who stuck it out for a month before being
ousted in turn by Dr Phan Huy Quat. By forcing the still-threatening
General Kanh to go abroad Quat managed to stay in office several
months.

At this point (May 1965) the Americans, despairing of leaving the
destruction of the NLF in such chaotic hands, brought in their own
combat teams. But they still needed the South Vietnamese army (such
as it was) for most combat operations. It was therefore felt that another
military commander as head of State would suit their purpose best.
Phan Huy Quat was deposed in favour of Nguyen Cao Ky, who offered
the further advantage of speaking good American. Thus eight adminis-
trations occupied a mere eighteen months. For the South Vietnamese
people this wild discontinuity, coming on top of Diem's reign of terror,
was the final disseverance from any sense of kinship with their government. What was the reality for the hard-pressed peasant who made up
ninety per cent of the population? The Americans and their Vietnamese
henchmen promised to save them from a 'Communist takeover'.

> This is a notion which to the Vietnamese peasant means absolutely
> nothing. The Vietcong never mention the subject of Communism.
> They don't present themselves as the exponents of a new ideology.
> The whole thing is infinitely more simple than that. Their political
> staff don't hold meetings of the peasants to conduct seminars in
> political theory. What they do is propose concrete solutions to
> concrete problems. These problems are not difficult to state. They
> are, in the order of their importance: the return of peace; the re-
> establishment of law and order; the better management of public
> affairs.[5]

Ho makes this point effectively in one of his addresses.[6]

---

[4] Suggestions have been put forward that Kennedy was assassinated for this
very reason; namely, that he was beginning to believe that the 'containment
of communism' was a mistaken policy. Such a belief was anathema to the
extreme Right.
[5] *The Situation in Vietnam* by Max Clos, written for Figaro Litteraire, and
later inserted in the Congressional Record (21 April 1965), pp. 7860/62.
[6] *To A Study Class*, 8 January 1967.

During the resistance against the French I came across some comrades resting beneath a banyan tree. They told me they'd just come
from a study class. 'What have you been studying?' I asked them.
'Karl Marx', they told me. 'Was it interesting?' 'Very interesting.'
'Did you understand it all?' Embarrassed, they at last replied, 'Dear
Uncle, there were some very difficult things that we couldn't understand.' Studies like that are not realistic.

Following Lenin's precepts, Ho had trained all his cadres in this simple,
direct and practical fashion. The NLF units had taken such lessons to
heart and they also hammered home the difference between conditions
north and south of the Parallel. In the north there was 'a real government, law and order and responsible people'. In the south, 'chaos,
anarchy and disorder . . . a continual turnover of important civil and
military officials who were killed, jailed, silenced, fired and recalled. . . .
The people chose those who had won the contest. Against this, bombs
and strafing meant nothing.'[7]
In February 1965, the United States Government, as a preparation
for full scale military action, had put its propaganda machine to work
with a 'white paper' relating in detail her reasons for entering the
contest:

South Vietnam is fighting for its life against a brutal campaign of
terror and armed attack inspired, directed, supplied and controlled
by the communist régime in Hanoi. This flagrant aggression has been
going on for years, but recently the pace has quickened and the
threat has now become active. The war in Vietnam is a new kind of
war, a fact as yet poorly understood in most parts of the world. Much
of the confusion that prevails in the thinking of many people and even
many governments, stems from this basic misunderstanding. For in
Vietnam a totally new brand of aggression has been loosed against
an independent people who want to make their own way in peace and
freedom. . . .

And so on for a total of 10,000 words. Even in the prevailing climate of
American chauvinism this paper was vigorously attacked.[8] U Thant,
who had been vainly trying to negotiate between Ho and Washington,[9]
put out a statement which finally convinced Johnson that the UN
Secretary-General was really on Ho's side. According to U Thant, it
was not the communist threat that had devastated Vietnam, but foreign
intervention. Burma had also had a communist threat, at times considerable. But the Burmese government, unlike the South Vietnam
government, had been careful not to ask for outside support, either
financial or military. Thus, Burma had not only avoided a full-scale
internal confrontation, but (despite an anti-communist stand) had kept
friendly relations with China, with whom she had a 1000-mile frontier.
Had she asked for outside help, Burma would have been divided like

[7] *The Situation in Vietnam.*
[8] See for example I. F. Stone in his weekly information sheet, reported in
Vietnam, History, Documents and Opinions, p. 335.
[9] See Lacouture, *op. cit.*, pp. 228/9.

Vietnam, and equally devastated.[10] President Johnson then came forth
with an additional 3,000 words along these lines: 'Every night before I
turn out the lights to sleep, I ask myself this question: Have I done
everything I can to unite this country [Vietnam]? Have I done everything I can to help unite the world, to try and bring peace and hope to
all the peoples of the world? Have I done enough?'[11] Ho, via Pham Van
Dong, put out a reply of a mere 300 words in which he stated his exact
requirements for 'uniting' his country; repeating the basic condition of
the Geneva treaty – that *all* foreign troops were to be barred from both
North and South – he insisted that the Vietnamese people in both zones
be allowed to settle their own affairs.[12]

The United States ignored these proposals and it was not until
1966 that Johnson aired his 'negotiating position' at a press conference, with fourteen points that are the essence of reasonableness;
but they were never subsequently put on record or conveyed to
Ho.[13]

Meanwhile, the United States had consistently buried all Ho's other
peace feelers, including one through U Thant in September 1964, in
which Ho offered to send a representative to meet the Americans in
Rangoon. Johnson had chosen to ignore this suggestion, and it was not
until almost a year later that the facts leaked out in the press. Faced
with this inconvenient disclosure, Secretary of State Dean Rusk
asserted that he had not been able to accept the move as genuine.[14] But
a different reason subsequently leaked: Secretary of Defence McNamara
had felt that the State of Vietnam, then undergoing not only a change
of dictators but also a Buddhist uprising, could not be further undermined by peace proposals. 'Though these facts came as a shock to most
Americans and created something of a crisis of confidence in the
government, a careful reading of *The New York Times* shows that the
United States has rejected no fewer than seven efforts to negotiate an
end of the war.'[15]

Despite this, Johnson declared at a press conference: 'There has
not been the slightest indication that the other side is interested
in negotiation or in unconditional discussion, although the United
States has made some dozen separate attempts to bring that
about.'[16]

As if to justify this statement, Rusk then publicized some apparently
genuine United States responses to Ho's new peace feelers; but at this
same time (as Ho disclosed, not without bitterness) American planes

[10] Statement to Press, 24 February 1965, summarized in *The US in Vietnam*
by George McTurnan Kahin and John W. Lewis, Dial Press, N.Y., 1967,
p. 410.

[11] For full text see *Vietnam, History, Documents and Opinions*, pp. 341–7.

[12] For full text see *op. cit.*, pp. 450/1.

[13] For a listing of the 14 points see *New York Times*, 2 January 1966, or
Vietnam, History, Documents and Opinions, p. 451.

[14] Reported in *The New York Times*, 17 November 1965.

[15] *Peace in Vietnam*, American Friends Service Committee, New York, 1967,
p. 50. The report goes on to describe these seven efforts, all substantiated
with dates and sources, p. 51.

[16] Quoted in *The New York Times* (and elsewhere), 13 July 1965.

were intensifying their bombing of the North.[17] A week or two later
the United States

> moved from irritated outbursts over U Thant's efforts for negotiations
> to a general appeal to the United Nations to use its good offices
> (though the United States has not formally laid the Vietnam problem
> before the United Nations as it was bound by the UN Charter to do
> before taking unilateral military action).[18]

Simultaneously Johnson stopped the bombing and sent representatives
to a dozen heads of state in a campaign to promote peace. This surprising switch seems to have been intended to refute the weight of
evidence disclosing former recalcitrance. Unfortunately this peace
offensive continued to ignore the real issue: no offer was made to withdraw the American troops, whose numbers went on increasing, while
the bombing in the south also intensified. Ho would have thus been
called upon to negotiate a peace that left out of account the National
Liberation Front. Even had he wished to do so, this would have been
impossible, since the NLF was then largely autonomous. Either
wilfully or through ignorance Johnson still refused to believe that the
'Vietcong' was anything more than a tool of Hanoi.

Thus the bombing was a second time resumed. This occasioned
protests almost everywhere, not only from official sources the world
over but from inside the United States. Particularly damaging to
Washington were the reports in *The New York Times* by Harrison
Salisbury, who revealed the 'widespread devastation of homes, schools,
churches, hospitals, shops, factories and whole villages.'[19] The United
States then insisted this bombing was a justified retaliation against
Hanoi's 'implacable aggression', and dismissed Ho's counter-charge
that since the two countries were not even at war it was a flagrant
violation of international law.

In the meantime Ho had sent a personal appeal to de Gaulle to make
further French efforts towards a settlement.[20] De Gaulle responded by
sending Sainteny on another mission. Ready to forget the incident of
the Hungarians, Ho received the Frenchman with the old cordiality.
But what was there to talk about? Sainteny had nothing new to offer
from the Americans; and Ho had already made his own position clear.
He did, however, soften this position by assuring Sainteny that his
demand for American withdrawal did not require immediate compliance, only their agreement to be out by a certain date. De Gaulle
followed this up, but the Americans would not then agree to any kind
of evacuation without prior withdrawal of the 'Hanoi forces'.[21]

---

[17] *The New York Times*, 21 December 1965. Ho's bitterness can be the more
readily understood when we remember that only a day earlier he had told
a British correspondent, James Cameron, that if the Americans stopped
the war he would 'roll out the red carpet for them'. Associated Press,
20 December 1965.

[18] *Peace in Vietnam*, p. 61.

[19] *ibid.*, p. 89.

[20] Reported in *Le Monde*, 1 February 1966.

[21] See Lacouture, *Ho Chi Minh*, pp. 236f.

As time passed, US combat troops were increased from a battalion to a division, from one division to five, from five to twenty, while the US air force dropped more bombs on the Vietnamese both North and South than on the whole of Europe during World War II. The policy of escalation was based upon John F. Kennedy's 'graduated response' devised during the Cuban missile crisis. It had succeeded there and was expected to succeed in Vietnam even though all the circumstances were different. To consider the most significant difference: Cuba had been far from Russia and near to the US but Vietnam was near to China and Russia and far from the US.[22] While Johnson went on talking about 'bringing Hanoi to their knees' a group of journalists and representatives of various international bodies (from Japan, France, Australia and the US) went to Hanoi to see the devastation for themselves. Afterwards they talked to the Hanoi leaders, including Ho. The American journalist, John Gerassi, takes us into the Presidential palace, where Pham Van Dong does the honours and greets them all by name. Then the President himself comes in, dressed in his usual 'people's suit':

> Ho, who was 77, also greeted us invividually. Pham made the introductions, remembering not only our names but our nationalities and our professions – and there were fourteen of us in all. Full of wit, with an easy style, Ho . . . joked about the fact that all of us came from former or current aggressor nations . . . and finally, very seriously, said, 'What you saw in the North must be multiplied by the hundreds for you to have an idea of what goes on in the South. Our intention is to fight to the end. Since we are offered either slavery to the US or victory, we have no alternative.'[23]

The anti-war protest at last pushed Johnson into political oblivion and replaced him with Nixon, a president whose election was based largely on his promise to extract America from the war. It was easy to promise, hard to fulfil:

> Today (1969) there are well over a million men fighting on our side.[24] United States air firepower is about 1000 to 1 over the enemy's. Our ground fire superiority is at least 10 to 1. The enemy has few tanks, practically no planes, no warships, and only a fraction of the material resources available to the US.[25]

In these terrible years from 1967 to 1969, Ho had little need to voice any of his own anti-American propaganda. Three out of four journalists who went to the war fronts came back either guiltily questioning or openly against this United States involvement in a war that made the

[22] See Henry Brandon, *Anatomy of Error*, Andre Deutsch, 1970, p. 162.
[23] *North Vietnam*, John Gerassi, George Allen & Unwin, 1968, p. 58.
[24] Of the SEATO nations, the US had persuaded Australia, New Zealand and the Philippines to contribute troops. France and Britain refused to do so, much embittering the Americans.
[25] William J. Lederer, *op. cit.*, p. 15.

French *sale guerre* look comparatively spotless. In addition to adverse press reports, book after book reflected the disillusionment.

This faraway war in defense of a people they hardly know, even to-day, has created deep chasms among adults and helped to trigger a rebellion among the young. It has destroyed many well-established assumptions. It has led to the abdication of the American President and the electoral defeat of his party, and has cruelly scarred the US reputation round the world. The war has undermined America's confidence in the judgement of their leaders, in their institutions, their military establishments, and their foreign policy. It has inflamed the young to the extent that they have begun to resist military service as perhaps never before in American history.[26]

The Pentagon put their propaganda snow machine to work with such frantic zeal that they finally bogged down under the weight of their own slush.

The corruption of language, of vision, and of sensibility which has risen like a poisonous ground fog from the Vietnam war sometimes produces its own parody. Probably the most well known was the explanation for the levelling of Ben Tre during the 1968 Tet offensive. It had to be destroyed, an American officer told reporters, *in order to save it.*[27]

This Tet offensive (February 1968), in which the National Liberation Front suddenly overran the American positions and penetrated to the heart of Saigon, was an even greater shock to American morale than the preceding revelation of subterfuge. Pictured coruscatingly on television screens it made a harrowing disclosure of American self-delusion and ultimately 'sealed Lyndon Johnson's political fate and forced the opening of the Paris talks, a veritable suit for peace for which the United States gave the required down payment: the limiting and then the halting of the bombing of North Vietnam.'[28]

Yet Johnson continued to assert that Ho did not really want peace; and to prove it would quote his opponent's remarks out of context. What he excluded was Ho's stipulation that *he did not want peace on United States terms*, which ignored the National Liberation Front and left a divided Vietnam with the South under a puppet régime. 'The Americans say we want this war to go on. How can they say such a thing? You have seen the country. You have seen the suffering which the raids have inflicted on our people. How can anyone want this war to continue? They leave us no alternative but to fight on.'[29]

In 1969 the new American President, Richard Nixon, had to substantiate, at least in part, his election pledge to get America out of the war, then killing up to 300 Americans a week. His plan was to teach the South Vietnamese how to fight in place of the American. In step with

[26] Henry Brandon, *op. cit.*, p. 150.
[27] Dale Minor, *The Information War*, p. 58, Hawthorne, NY, 1970.
[28] *ibid.*, p. 71.
[29] Felix Greene, quoting Ho in a radio broadcast, 2 March 1969.

their successful tuition, the American troops would be withdrawn. Ho
was at last able to tell his people, in an address on 20 July 1969, 'The
Americans are beaten' instead of the customary 'The Americans will
be beaten.'

But the victory was still on the distant horizon and Ho was now
seventy-nine years old. At this time, with what seems prescience, he
wrote his official testament: 'a few lines before I go to join the venerable
Karl Marx, V. I. Lenin and the other old revolutionaries'. Promising
his people the unified and independent country to which he had devoted
his life, he added: 'When I'm dead, I hope no time and money will be
wasted on any elaborate funeral arrangements.'[30]

And as things turned out, the sun of victory rose too slowly for Ho
to see it reach its meridian. Having lived just long enough to see the
first of the Americans decamp, he died 3 September 1969. In regard
to world obituaries, *de mortuis nil nisi bonum* has seldom been more
generally applied. Reporting the universal tribute, *The New York Times*
wrote of 'the veneration and respect which even his bitterest opponents
could not help feeling for the frail and wispy "Uncle Ho".'[31] *Time*
magazine found themselves, for the fourth spectacular occasion, putting
his face on their cover,[32] and rendering this man they had often designated as America's number-one enemy this tribute:

> Ho Chi Minh's life was dedicated to the creation of a united Vietnam,
> free from foreign control, and the 19 million people of his tortured
> land suffered mightily from his total devotion to that vision. Even so,
> they affectionately knew him as 'Bac Ho' (Uncle Ho). So did many
> in the South. No national leader alive to-day has stood so stubbornly
> or so long before the enemy's guns.[33]

It was not Ho's destiny to die from those guns, but from a heart attack.
For the first time in fifty years he was compelled to leave the welfare of
his people entirely to the care of others. We may justly grant him an
epitaph that Livy gave to Hannibal: 'His iron will humbled the mountain peaks.'

[30] *President Ho Chi Minh's Testament*, Foreign Languages Publishing House,
    Hanoi, 1969.
[31] 7 September 1969.
[32] 12 September 1969.
[33] *ibid.*

Appendix A
Language

The controversy about 'modernizing' and thus simplifying the Chinese script (which is – or was – employed for Vietnamese, Japanese and every Chinese dialect) seems to epitomize the gulf between Western and Eastern concepts; or, more specifically, between the modern western world of science, efficiency and 'progress' and the ancient eastern world of art, mysticism and 'no-progress'.

A literate Chinese, of whatever area, speaking whatever dialect (and some are as different as French is from English), shares with the literate Vietnamese and Japanese, the heritage of a written language so intellectually fascinating and visually charming that in itself it constitutes what might well be called the highest single manifestation of true human progress. Every character is in itself an art-form: a painting, an abstraction, a concept; perfect in form, explicit in meaning, with a balance, strength, harmony, lucidity and intellectual force that enable the Chinese artist not only to employ his highest skill in rendering the character but to know that what he renders can make its impact on scores of millions of his fellows: even the illiterate see and understand the characters everywhere written up on shop-fronts, hanging signs, proclamations, New Year and other 'good-luck' scrolls, executed in large bold strokes, often with skill and artistry. We have only to consider a few individual characters to see the gulf between our own visually unrewarding roman script and the Chinese character script. Take the English word 'dawn', for example: the best we can say about it is that it has a quite nice sound; but (except for our heritage of memory associations) no nicer than 'lawn' or 'fawn' or a hundred other four-letter words of more mundane significance. Compare this word 'dawn' with the related Chinese character, which, in six strokes (taking rather less time to write than 'dawn') shows us, in an 'abstract' that Picasso could be proud of, the sun rising above the horizon.

To consider some less pictorial examples: the Chinese character for 'good' shows, in a mere seven strokes, a woman and a child; for 'friendship' we are shown two hands coming together; and for 'peace' we have a woman under a roof. These beautiful concepts are enhanced by being exquisitely contained within a square while yet retaining total form and balance. Any single one, executed by a master calligraphist, might take its place amongst the world's masterpieces of art.

This, then, is what the French threw out (aided by the contemporary Vietnamese) in favour of our little roman squiggles. Let us, however, do them this justice: in the cause of 'progress' there are a dozen good reasons in favour of making the change. Already Chairman Mao Tse-tung, himself a declared opponent of the kind of 'progress' cherished in the West, has decided that 'Chinese characters must be reformed, and that reform will take the form of the rest of the world – Romanization'. (Quoted in *The Times*, 8 April 1972.)

Appendix B
Poems from Ho's *Prison Diary*

It is almost impossible to translate Chinese poems: too much of their quality is inherent in the characters themselves. The subtleties of style, rhythm and form are also lost. Only someone who is himself a poet may hope to give us something of the flavour. The following selection is from the official translated version of Ho's *Prison Diary*.[1]

Prison Meals

At every meal, only one bowl of red rice,
Without vegetables, without salt, and even no broth to go with it.
Those who get food brought in to them can sometimes eat their fill.
But, without help from outside the jail, we groan with hunger.

Cold Night

In the cold autumn nights, without mattress, without blankets,
Lying with back curled round and legs folded up close,
I try in vain to sleep. The moonlight on the plantains
Increases the sense of cold, and through the window-bars
The Great Bear draws up alongside and looks in.

Death of a Man Imprisoned for Gambling

Nothing remained of him but skin and bone.
Misery, cold and hunger were the end of him.
Only last night he slept close to my side,
But this morning he is gone to the Nine Springs' Country.

The Water Ration

Each of us has a ration of half a basin of water
For washing or brewing tea, according as each may choose:
If you want to wash your face, then you must go without brewing tea:
If you want a drink of tea, then you have to go without washing your face.

Transferred to Tian Pao on 'Double Tenth' Day

Every house was festooned with flowers and with lanterns.
On the national day, the whole country went wild with joy,
But on that very day, I was placed in chains and transferred:
The wind remains contrary to the flight of the eagle.

[1] Foreign Languages Publishing House, Hanoi 1965 (translated by Aileen Palmer).

Arrival at Tian Pao

To-day I walked fifty-three kilometres,
My clothes are wet through, my shoes are in tatters,
And all night long, without a place to lie down,
I wait for the next day's coming, on the edge of a cess-pool.

On the way to Nanning

The supple rope has now been replaced with iron fetters.
At every step they jingle as though I wore jade rings.
In spite of being a prisoner, accused of being a spy,
I move with all the dignity of an ancient government official!

At the End of Four Months

'One day in jail is equal to a thousand years outside it . . .'
How right were the ancients, expressing it in those words!
Four months leading a life in which there is nothing human
Have aged me more than ten years.
Yes: in a whole four months I have never eaten my fill,
In four months I have never changed my clothes, and in four months
I have never taken a bath.
So: I have lost a tooth, my hair has grown grey,
And, lean and black as a demon gnawed by hunger,
I am covered with scabies.

Fortunately
Being stubborn and patient, never yielding an inch,
Though physically I suffer, my spirit is unshaken.

Twilight

Now the wind's edge is sharpened on mountain rocks.
The spear of cold pierces the branches of trees.
The gong from a far-off pagoda hastens
The traveller's steps and boys are playing flutes
As they drive the buffaloes home across the twilight.

Appendix C
Ho's Handwriting

In the course of agent-assessment I found the most useful and accurate guide to character was graphology, which I had studied for that purpose. The following analysis of Ho's handwriting was made without any prior concept of the man we were dealing with. Analytically I would find nothing to change in my analysis to-day; but were I making it with my present knowledge of the writer's identity I could scarcely dare credit his simplicity unless I also remembered that it was Ho's best friend and military right arm, Vo Nguyen Giap, who insisted that his leader appeared 'so simple that nothing particular could be found in him'. (Quoted in *Days with Ho Chi Minh*, p. 175.)

The essential features are simplicity, desire to make everything clear, remarkable self-control. Knows how to keep a secret. Neat, orderly, unassuming, no interest in dress or outward show. Self confident and dignified. Gentle but firm. Loyal, sincere and generous, would make a good friend. Outgoing, gets along with anyone. Keen analytical mind, difficult to deceive. Shows readiness to ask questions. Good judge of character. Full of enthusiasm, energy, initiative. Conscientious; painstaking attention to detail. Imaginative, interested in aesthetics, particularly literature. Good sense of humour.

Faults: diplomatic to the point of contriving. Could be moody and obstinate.

Appendix D
Author's note

The story of Fate's intervention in my further relationship with Ho is this: while in Hong Kong in 1947 I wrote a play about Vietnam (*Fireeaters*), subsequently produced at Stratford East by Joan Littlewood. As a result some Vietnamese students urged me to go to Hanoi. Since passing through French lines was likely to prove difficult Ho wrote that he would try to send someone to meet me. While I was waiting, my work in the theatre took me to London. Soon afterwards, the American Embassy asked me to call in about a passport formality (I am a British-born American citizen). When I handed over my passport to the Vice-Consul he then informed me I should not get it back except stamped 'For return to U.S. only'. No reasons were given. Then came a new twist: it seemed that in 1941 while we were off at the battle-fronts a law had been passed in the U.S. whereby naturalized citizens who subsequently stayed in the country of their birth for more than three years were liable to lose their citizenship. Through the workings of this law I found myself not only without a passport but Stateless. During the next eighteen years I applied several times first for British nationality (which had been forfeited when I became an American citizen) then for Irish. Despite strict fulfilment of all requirements I was turned down each time with no reasons given and no chance of appeal. Thus my travelling was severely limited; to go as far as Vietnam was impossible. One day in 1970 an American tourist passing through the Irish fishing village where I live happened to mention that this law of 1941 had been thrown out by the U.S. Supreme Court as unconstitutional: I needed only to apply for re-instatement. When I did this, *mirabile dictu*, I shortly found myself again an American citizen and was issued with a US passport. My travel problems were over; but Ho was then dead.

Appendix E
The Geneva Agreements

If politics is the art of the possible, international politics, or statecraft, is the art of the impossible. Because there is seldom any continuity in national governments or national policy, what is true for a nation to-day may be false to morrow. Ho was able to recognize what Spinoza was at pains to teach us: that the apparent bad faith of nations is not a reflection of the dishonesty of individuals, but is inherent in the requirements of statecraft. An individual can afford to have 'principles'; a nation seldom can. The government of a nation is required to consider the welfare of its people at that particular moment, and is not required to consider principles, rights and wrongs, the world's welfare, any other people's welfare, or even the commitments of its predecessors. This is why we find men of apparent integrity such as Eden and Blum forced into ignoring their obligations. Spinoza states the case succinctly:

> A treaty will be valid only so long as the occasion of it, namely, the danger that had to be provided against or the advantage which had to be secured, continues in existence. Experience also amply confirms this. For although different States make agreements not to do one another any injury, they still try, as far as possible, to prevent their allies increasing in power. And they do not put faith in any mere promises, but require to see clearly the end and the advantage for the sake of which the other nation made the treaty. Otherwise they fear treachery, and not unnaturally. For who except a fool, ignorant of the rights of a State, is satisfied with mere promises from a ruler; seeing that a ruler has supreme power and the right to act as he pleases, and is bound to treat the safety and welfare of his own State as the supreme law of his conduct.[1]

Additionally, we find other men, no doubt of equal integrity, such as Eisenhower and Kennedy, making decisions later to be considered not only mistaken but abhorrent.

> A nation's right to go to war for whatever seems to itself just and sufficient cause is one of the inalienable rights which no State can give up. It is one of the laws of its own integrity and existence. For there is no one who will care for, or maintain, its honour and place, if it does not do so itself. It may make war whenever it thinks the consequences or results to be gained by doing so will render it more secure, strong, or internally at one with itself. And in going to war it does not need the consent, approval, or warrant of any other State or authority. The only check upon the abuse of this power is that which comes from the inevitable calamities and uncertainties of war

[1] Spinoza, *Tractatus Theologico-Politicus*, chapter 16.

itself, the weakening of the nation's resources which it produces, and the diversion of its energies into unprofitable channels which a condition of war gives rise to.[2]

Whether or not Ho had ever read Spinoza he certainly understood these concepts. Thus he was able to work inside the comity of nations (whenever permitted) without either misplaced hopes or embittered disillusionment. This carried him through no matter what appalling reverses. He himself was fortunate in not only being identified with his people from start to finish but being a continuing government with a continuing policy. The policy was simple enough: to help his people gain their unity and independence. Such a cause was obviously just. But justice no more than principles can enter into statecraft. Ho learned to accept the reality of *jus est in armis*.

What particularly distinguished the Vietnamese leader as a statesman was his inclination to work from the heart rather than from the head. Instinctively employing the *shu* of Confucius, he aroused a vibration in the hearts of people everywhere. Not only did he win the affection of his own young people, but in the end he won over thousands of young Americans. Convinced that, no matter how savage the conflict, humanity does not declare war on humanity, he remained open to the concept that all men are brothers. In that concept lies the essence of Hochiminity.

[2] Paraphrase of Spinoza's text from the same work, given in *Spinoza's Political and Ethical Philosophy*, Robert A. Duff, James Maclehose, 1903, p. 458.

Chronological Table

1000 BC	The tribe of Giao-chi invade Vietnam from China
3rd c. BC	Chinese invade in bulk
208 BC	First Kingdom of Vietnam
939 AD	Chinese rule overthrown
15th c.	Le Loi establishes the Le Dynasty
1802	Nguyen Anh proclaims himself Emperor Gia-long of Vietnam
1859–83	Conquest of Indo-China by the French
1890	Ho Chi Minh born
1900	His mother dies
1909	Journeys south to Cochin China
1911	Sails off to sea.
1912?	Sails to American ports
1913/14	Goes to London
1915?	Visits Liverpool
1917	Goes to Paris
1919	Petitions Versailles Peace Conference
1920	Addresses Tours Conference; joins French Communist Party
1923/24	Goes to Moscow; takes part in Fifth Congress of the Communist International
1925	Goes to China with Borodin
1926	Organizes Thanh Nien
1928	Goes to Siam; visits Moscow
1930	Organizes the Indo-Chinese Communist Party in Hong Kong; Yen Bay Mutiny staged by VNQDD Xo-Viet uprising inspired by ICP
1931	Ho arrested in Hong Kong
1933	Goes to Moscow
1934	Attends Lenin School
1935	Takes part in Seventh Congress of the Communist International; perhaps goes to Macao for Indo-Chinese Communist Party First Congress
1936	Popular Front Government in France
1937	Japanese invasion of China. Chiang Kai-shek makes truce with Chinese Communists
1938	Ho convalesces in Sochi
1939	Goes to Yenan and south-west to Kunming World War II begins in Europe
1940	Fall of France Japanese troops, with French co-operation, occupy Indo-China
1941	Ho re-enters Vietnam from China, founds the Vietminh at Bac Bo; Japanese attack Pearl Harbor; US enters war
1942	Re-enters China, is arrested, imprisoned

1944   Released, agreement reached with Chinese Nationalists; Dong Minh Hoi founded

1945 Feb. Ho sets off for Kunming, meets Lt. Shaw, a rescued US pilot

Mar. Japanese coup in Indo-China against French

Apr. AGAS-Ho hook-up; he returns to Vietnam as 'agent'

July Potsdam Conference, Indo-China to be divided into two zones

Aug. World War II ends, Vietminh take over, declare Independence; Indo-Chinese Communist Party disbanded

Sep. Chinese occupy North Vietnam, British take over South

1946 Mar. French recognize Ho's Republic of Vietnam as a free State

May D'Argenlieu sets up puppet 'Republic of Cochin China'

June Ho in France to finalize settlement; returns with '*modus vivendi*'

Dec. War breaks out between French and Vietminh

1949 Mar. France establishes puppet State of Vietnam under Bao Dai

Oct. Communists win struggle in China

1950 Jan. Ho's Democratic Republic of Vietnam recognized first by Mao's People's Republic of China, then by Soviet Union

May The US begins military aid to French in Vietnam

1951 Feb. Founding of the Lao Dong

1953 Mar. Death of Stalin leads to subsequent Geneva Conference

1954 May French defeated at Dien Bien Phu

July Ngo Dinh Diem made Head of State in South Vietnam; Geneva Treaty signed, Vietnam split at 17th Parallel

Oct. Eisenhower offers aid to Diem

1955 Jan. First American military supplies arrive in Saigon; Diem rejects proposed elections

1956   French forces leave South, deadline passes for elections; Peasant discontent in North Vietnam forcibly put down; Land Reform Campaign fails

1957   Diem's campaign of terror stirs first resistance in South

1959   Ho decides North must help this resistance movement

1960   Le Duan appointed Party Secretary National Liberation Front set up in South

1961 Nov. Kennedy offers increased military aid to Diem

Dec. US White Paper states United States intentions

1962   International Control Commission censures US and Diem régime for military activity; censures Ho's government for aiding NLF

1963 Nov. Diem assassinated; Kennedy assassinated

1964 Jan. Coup *d'état* by General Nguyen Kanh

Aug. Tonkin Gulf incident; US attacks DRV mainland bases Buddhist uprising against Kanh régime

Sept. U Thant makes Ho's negotiation offer to US

Nov. Johnson re-elected

1965 Feb. US White Paper prepares for increased military action

April Johnson's 'Johns Hopkins' speech; DRV's 'Four Points'

May First US combat troops in action; First pause in US bombing; Nguyen Kao Ky appointed 'Head of State'

Nov. Massive protests in US to end war

Dec. Second pause in US bombing

1966 Jan. Ho appeals to de Gaulle; Sainteny goes to Hanoi; Johnson
           airs his 'Fourteen Points'; bombing of North resumed
     Oct. Johnson's Manila Conference to promote outside approval
1967 Jan. Salisbury's *New York Times* reports shock America
1968 Feb. Tet offensive reveals full weakness of US and South Vietnam;
           public pressure in US to get out of Vietnam
     Nov. Nixon elected President, promises graduated withdrawal
1969 May   First US troop withdrawal
     Sept. Ho dies

Bibliography

American Friends Service Committee *Peace in Vietnam* Friends Book Centre, London 1967

Azeau, Henri *Ho Chi Minh, Dernière Chance* Flammarion, Paris 1950

Betts, Raymond F. *Assimilation and Association in French Colonial Theory 1890–1914* Columbia University Press, New York 1961

Burchett, Wilfred *North of the Seventeenth Parallel* People's Publishing House, Delhi 1956

Mekong Upstream Languages Publishing House, Moscow 1959

The Furtive Way International Publishers, New York 1963

Vietnam, Inside Story of the Guerilla War International Publishers, New York 1965

Buttinger, Joseph *Vietnam* Frederick A. Praeger, New York 1969

Chesneaux, Jean *The Vietnamese Nation* Australian Current Books, Sydney 1966

Days with Ho Chi Minh Foreign Languages Publishing House, Hanoi 1965

Devillers, Philippe *Histoire du Vietnam de 1940 à 1952* Editions de Seuil, Paris 1952

Duncanson, Dennis J. *Government and Revolution in Vietnam* Oxford University Press, London 1968

Fall, Bernard B. *The Two Vietnams* Frederick A. Praeger, New York/London 1964

Viet-Nam Witness Praeger, New York/London 1966

Gettleman, Marvin E. (ed.) *Vietnam: History, Documents and Opinions on a Major World Crisis* Penguin Books, London 1966

Halberstam, David *The Making of a Quagmire* Random House, New York 1964

Ho Barrie & Jenkins, London 1971

Hammer, Ellen J. *The Struggle for Indochina* Stanford University Press, USA 1954

Ho Chi Minh *Selected Works* 4 vols. Foreign Languages Publishing House, Hanoi 1960–2

Prison Diary Foreign Languages Publishing House, Hanoi 1965

Hoang Van Chi *From Colonialism to Communism* Pall Mall Press, London 1964

Honey, P. J. *Genesis of a Tragedy* Ernest Benn, London 1968

(ed. P. J. Honey) *North Vietnam Today* Praeger, New York/London 1962

Kahin, George McT. (ed.) *Government and Politics of South-East Asia* Cornell University Press, Ithiaca, N.Y. 1964

Lacouture, Jean *Vietnam Between Two Truces* Random House, New York 1966

Ho Chi Minh Allen Lane The Penguin Press, London 1968

Lederer, William J. *The Anguished American* Gollancz, London 1969

Le Duan *On the Socialist Revolution in Vietnam* 2 vols. Foreign Languages Publishing House, Hanoi 1968

Lenin, V. I. *Selected Works* 2 vols. Languages Publishing House,
    Moscow 1952
  Imperialism Languages Publishing House, Moscow 1947
Murti, B. S. N. *Vietnam Divided* Asia Publishing House, New York 1964
Mus, Paul *Vietnam: Sociologie d'une guerre* Editions du Seuil, Paris 1952
Pike, Douglas *Viet Cong: The Organisation and Techniques of the
    National Liberation Front of South Vietnam* MIT Press, Cambridge,
    Mass. 1966
Raskin, Marcus G., and Fall, Bernard B. (eds.) *The Vietnam Reader*
    Vintage Books, New York 1965
Sainteny, Jean *Histoire d'une Paix Manquée* Amiot-Dumont, Paris 1953
  Face à Ho Chi Minh Editions Seghers, Paris 1970
Shaplen, Robert *The Lost Revolution* André Deutsch, London 1966
  The Road From War André Deutsch, London 1971
Snow, Edgar *The Other Side of the River: Red China Today* Gollancz,
    London 1963
Tanham, George K. *Communist Revolutionary Warfare: The Vietminh
    in Indochina* Praeger, New York/London 1961
Truong Chinh *Primer for Revolt* Praeger, New York/London 1963
Vo Nguyen Giap *Dien Bien Phu* Foreign Languages Publishing House,
    Hanoi 1962
  People's War, People's Army Drager, London 1962
Warbey, William *Vietnam: The Truth* The Merlin Press, London 1965

Index